CAMBRIDGE SCIENCE EDUCATION SERIES
Series editor Richard Ingle

£5.50

Assessment in Science

Richard Kempa

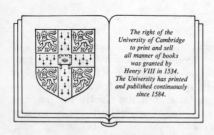

The right of the
University of Cambridge
to print and sell
all manner of books
was granted by
Henry VIII in 1534.
The University has printed
and published continuously
since 1584.

CAMBRIDGE UNIVERSITY PRESS

Cambridge

London   New York   New Rochelle

Melbourne   Sydney

D1227533

Published by the Press Syndicate of the University of Cambridge
The Pitt Building, Trumpington Street, Cambridge CB2 1RP
32 East 57th Street, New York, NY 10022, USA
10 Stamford Road, Oakleigh, Melbourne 3166, Australia

© Cambridge University Press 1986

First published 1986

Printed in Great Britain at the University Press, Cambridge

Library of Congress catalogue card number: 85-22429

British Library cataloguing in publication data

Kempa, Richard
    Assessment in science. – (Cambridge science education series)
    1. Science – Great Britain – Ability testing
    2. Science – Study and teaching – Great Britain
    I. Title
    507'.1041   Q183.4.G7

ISBN 0 521 27863 5

The author

Richard Kempa is Professor of Education at the University of Keele. A chemist by initial training, he specialises in Science Education and is particularly interested in a wide range of issues relating to the learning of scientific concepts and to instructional strategies in science education. Professor Kempa has had substantial involvement in examining and assessment work. He previously held the positions of Chief Examiner and Moderator for the University of London GCE Chemistry examination and, in these capacities, took a leading role in the development of new examination techniques by that Board. Since 1982, he has been a member of the Science Steering Committee of the Assessment of Performance Unit.

The series editor

Dr Richard Ingle is Lecturer in Science Education at the University of London Institute of Education. He graduated in the physical sciences at Durham University and then taught science in secondary schools for a period of fourteen years in Scotland, England and Uganda. He subsequently held posts in chemical education at Makerere University College, Uganda, and at the Centre for Science Education, Chelsea College, University of London. During the 1970s he undertook an evaluation of Nuffield Chemistry and subsequently became general editor of the revised Nuffield Chemistry series. He was for a time education adviser at the Ministry of Overseas Development. His current interests include the pre-service and in-service education of science teachers, cultural aspects of science education, and the probing of learning difficulties faced by pupils in using mathematics in the course of their science education.

DS

CONTENTS

Acknowledgements

The author and the publisher would like to thank the following for permission to reproduce copyright material:

Chapter 4, examples 1-5 DES *Science at Ages 13 and 15*: Sample questions, reproduced with the permission of the Controller of Her Majesty's Stationery Office.

Other copyright holders are acknowledged in the text.

Cover photograph by Sally and Richard Greenhill
Cover design by Andrew Bonnett

PREFACE

Examinations and assessment form an integral part of the educational process as a whole. They are used for a variety of diverse purposes, ranging from the grading of students and the measuring of their attainment, at one end of the spectrum, to controlling and maintaining educational standards, at the other.

The examination and assessment area, like the curriculum area in general, is one in which major changes have been brought about in recent years, and where further major changes are likely to take place in the future. In science education in particular, these changes have had a significant effect on educational pratice, e.g. through the adoption of a variety of examination and assessment techniques and the increasing teacher involvement in public examinations. The current trend towards 'graded assessment' and 'profiling' indicates further changes ahead.

The purpose of this book is to present a concise but scholarly account of the context and nature of examinations and assessment in science education, and of the problems and issues relating to them. The general orientation is towards the secondary-education level and this defines the broad readership at whom this book is aimed: practising science teachers, and students undergoing inservice and preservice teacher training. As far as possible, technical issues relating to examinations and assessment have not been discussed, but references have been made throughout the text to research articles and other documents, including Higher Degree theses, concerned with issues of assessment in science education. This should enable readers to follow up any points of particular interest to them.

In any appraisal of assessment in science education, the work by the Science Monitoring teams of the Assessment of Performance Unit (APU) merits special attention. For several years, these teams (located at Chelsea College, University of London, and the University of Leeds, respectively) have done outstanding work in the development and evaluation of new assessment procedures for the purpose of monitoring pupils' performance in science. Frequent reference has been made to this here, but the reader is encouraged to consult the original APU publications whenever possible.

Keele, 1985   Richard Kempa

Examinations and Assessment in Context

Examinations and assessments are an integral component of our education structure. They are conducted, both formally and informally, at practically all levels of education and serve a variety of different functions.

In the narrow sense, examinations and assessments may be thought of as having predominantly educational purposes. For example, we may use them in order:

– to assess students' attainments at the end of a course or study programme;
– to evaluate diagnostically students' academic progress and/or learning difficulties;
– to estimate students' aptitudes, possibly for the purpose of assigning them to different courses or teaching sets;
– to evaluate the effectiveness of an educational programme or curriculum.

Many of the examinations and assessments regularly conducted by teachers and schools on an 'internal' basis tend to fulfil one or more of these 'educational' functions.

Other examinations, e.g. those conducted 'externally' by the recognised examining boards and certain professional associations, likewise have a primary educational purpose: to assess the attainment of a student at the end of a course of study. However, we may also identify for them a range of functions which does not fall directly within the scope of educational concerns. This includes, for example:

– the use of examinations (and examination results) as instruments of selection for access to higher education, entry into employment and admission to the professions;
– the use of examinations as a means of defining the content and orientation of the curriculum and, linked with this,
– the maintenance of educational standards.

These latter functions arise from the societal role that is associated with the majority of public and professional examinations and have contributed significantly to the prominent position that these examinations occupy in our education system. Some of these functions and the effects deriving therefrom will be examined later in this chapter.

An Historical Perspective on Examinations

Our present system of public examinations is the result of an evolution that has been in progress for well over a century. The Historians of education generally regard the report of the Northcote–Trevelyan Commission of 1853 on entry to the British civil service as the most significant event at the beginning of the evolutionary process:[1] it led to the introduction of a competitive examination, on the basis of which recruitment to the civil service was determined. Further, similar developments followed: the military colleges of Sandhurst and Woolwich introduced competitive entrance examinations in the 1870s.

Universities, likewise, had set up examination boards to conduct examinations as a means of controlling the admission of students. The Oxford Delegacy of Local Examinations, established in 1858, was the first of these, but Cambridge soon followed suit. The initial intention associated with these examinations was the external assessment of the quality of education provided by the public and grammar schools (the latter in particular had considerably increased in number during the first half of the nineteenth century). But the focus of the examinations soon shifted from the school to individual students, as is indicated by the issue, from 1877 onwards, of examination certificates to individual students.

The next significant step was taken by the University of London through the establishment, in 1900, of a new Matriculation Examination to serve both as a school leaving examination and as a university entrance examination. This and other examinations, also developed during the late nineteenth century, readily found acceptance and widespread use for selection purposes in a variety of situations, e.g. local government and clerical occupations.

The powerful influence over school examinations and, hence, the school curriculum, that the universities began to exert in the second half of the last century, can only be understood when one realises that the State itself had failed to establish a central body to be responsible for school examinations. The establishment of such a body had been recommended as early as 1868 by a Schools Inquiry Commission (the Taunton Commission),[2] but no action was taken. Under these circumstances, the universities – by instituting their own school examinations – clearly filled an important gap. Not surprisingly, since this development was uncoordinated, the result was the provision of a multiplicity of external examinations that frequently reflected the academic values and orientations prevalent in the universities, but not the real educational needs of the pupils. As Lawton expressed it aptly: 'The age of school examinations controlled by university boards had begun'.[3]

The first successful attempt at creating a coordinated examination system was made in 1917 and led to the establishment of two new examinations for secondary schools: the School Certificate for pupils of age 16 years and the Higher School Certificate for 18-year olds. These examinations were still administered by universities, but they were now monitored by a national body, the Secondary Schools Examinations Council, which consisted of representatives from local authorities, the teaching profession and the universities. The School Certificate examination system thus introduced remained in operation until it was replaced, in 1951, by the General Certificate of Education (GCE) examination.

The abandonment of the School Certificate system was itself the consequence of major criticisms of its structure and effects. In the main, these arose from the fact that the examination for the 16-year old students was a 'group'-type examination that required them to gain passes in five subjects, including a science/mathematics subject, a humanities subject and a foreign language. One effect of this requirement was that school curricula tended to be strongly biased towards these subjects, to the exclusion or neglect of the arts and practical subjects. Another point of criticism stemmed from the need to pass either a science or mathematics subject: this was thought to be particularly unfair on female pupils. As the result of considerable pressure, this specific requirement was abandoned in 1938.

The main change brought about by the GCE system, compared with its predecessor, was the replacement of the group-examination requirement for students at age 16 years by a subject-based structure (at the Ordinary (O) Level of the GCE). The Advanced (A) Level GCE examination broadly retained all major characteristics of the Higher School Certificate examination, which was already a subject-based examination. Like the School Certificate examination, the GCE O-level examination was aimed primarily at pupils in grammar and public schools, viz. the 'top' 25–30% of pupils in their age group. The prestige of the new examination was such that soon many of the secondary modern schools were also entering candidates for the GCE examination, often inappropriately, whilst other secondary modern school pupils were now prepared for examinations that had been introduced by bodies such as the Royal Society of Arts, the College of Preceptors and others.

The emergence of these new examinations designed specifically for the 'non-academic' pupils, soon led to a multiplicity of external examinations similar to that which had existed at the beginning of the century, prior to the establishment of the School Certificate structure. It clearly called for some rationalisation and this was brought about by the establishment in 1963 of the Certificate of Secondary Education (CSE). Like GCE O-level examinations, CSE examinations are aimed primarily at the 16+ age group, although they cater for a lower ability group (30th to 60th

3

percentile and beyond). They too are subject-based but, unlike the former, are conducted and administered by regional examination boards which are controlled by teachers and not the university sector.

The impact of the CSE examination system has been considerable. It led to a substantial increase in the number (and percentage) of pupils taking formal public examinations and receiving recognised qualifications. It provided teachers with far more autonomy in the sphere of syllabus and examination design than had ever been the case before, albeit in relation to pupils of lower ability than those proceeding to O-level examinations.

The fact that the top grade of the CSE examination became officially recognised as being equivalent to a GCE O-level pass grade contributed significantly to the status of the new examination. However, it also led to a situation where CSE syllabuses (and examinations) were often little different from the established O-level syllabuses in the same subject (which itself enhanced the acceptability of the new examination). Even so, the CSE examination did not gain parity of esteem with the O-level GCE examination. Nuttall refers to the divisiveness of the dual system of examining at the 16+ age and states:

The effect of the dual system within the comprehensive school was to create grammar and secondary modern streams. Children had to be categorized into GCE and CSE groups, often at the beginning of the fourth year; not only did this categorization fail to match any natural division between the aspirations or abilities of the children, but it also created organizational and timetabling problems. To provide a safety net, many schools entered borderline candidates for both GCE and CSE, putting a severe burden on just those pupils who were having difficulty with the GCE course.[4]

Recognising these and other problems arising from the dual examination structure, the Schools Council proposed in 1970 that 'there should be a single examination system at the age of 16+' and commissioned a number of studies to investigate the feasibility of a unified examination system. (The Schools Council had been established by the Department of Education and Science in 1964 to oversee and coordinate educational development in relation to the school sector of education.) Following the evaluation of these studies in 1975, the Schools Council made a firm recommendation to the Department of Education and Science (DES) for a common system of examining at 16+. In response to these recommendations, the DES instituted in the following year a further study of this issue, under the chairmanship of Sir James Waddell.

The Waddell Committee's report,[5] published in 1978, made recommendations for a much stronger central coordination of the examination system and for the development of nationally agreed performance criteria to feature in these examinations. Following protracted debates, these proposals were accepted by the DES and formed the foundations of recent and current development work in the examinations field:

i The decision by the Secretary of State for Education to introduce a single system of examination at 16+ (the General Certificate in Secondary Education (GCSE) examination to be introduced in 1988), to replace the current GCE O-level/CSE structure.

ii The development, by the GCE and CSE boards through a joint Committee of National Criteria for 16+ Examinations in all major subjects.[6]

iii The development of detailed sets of 'graded objectives' for use in the award of achievement grades on a criterion-referenced basis.

Some of the issues arising from this work are taken up and discussed in later chapters.

Examinations as Instruments of Curriculum Control

In contrast to the majority of European (and other) countries, the English (and Welsh) education system is decentralised. This means that the responsibility for, e.g. the provision of education, the employment of teachers and the curriculum itself does not rest with a central agency (for example, the DES as the Ministry responsible for all matters of education), but lies with the Local Education Authorities. Normally though, decisions about the curriculum are not made at the local authority level, but are instead reached within individual schools. Hence, the teaching staff of a school can, at least in principle, contribute to a considerable extent to the determination of its school curriculum.

In practice, the freedom of secondary schools in England and Wales to determine their own curricula is severely restricted as a result of the external control of the formal school leaving examinations. The demands of these examinations, laid down in the examination syllabuses published by the examination boards, effectively define the content of courses offered by the schools and also have a significant influence on the teaching styles and strategies employed by teachers. Through this, an extensive 'indirect' control of the curriculum and of curricular decision-making is brought about, notwithstanding the fact that no formal external imposition of detailed curriculum requirements exists in the English secondary-school system.

Table 1.1 presents an abridged analysis of the effects and influences of examination structure and requirements on curricular decision-making within education institutions. As may be seen from this, even in situations where the general examination requirements are laid down by external agencies, it is possible for the actual structure and content of examinations to be controlled externally as well as internally. The external mode of control is, of course, exemplified by the wide range of 'standard' (Mode 1) GCE and CSE examinations that is offered by the various examination boards. Mode 3 CSE examinations, by comparison,

Table 1.1. Effect and influence of different examination structures on curricular decisions

Form of control of examination requirements	Control of the structure and content of examinations	Effect on internal, i.e. school-based, curriculum decisions
External (e.g. through school authorities, education ministries, university examining boards)	*External* (i.e. examinations are devised, conducted and evaluated by agencies external to the school)	Form, structure and content of the curriculum and teaching methods are extensively influenced by the examination requirements. Through this, a strong 'indirect' control of the curriculum by the external agency results.
	Internal (i.e. examinations are devised, administered and evaluated from within the school)	The indirect influence of the external agency on curricular decisions is reduced, compared with the above situation. Therefore, schools enjoy extensive freedom to develop their own courses and curricula, as long as these are in accord with the policies laid down by the external agency.
Internal (The teaching institution carries full responsibility for and freedom to decide about learning aims and objectives, and examination requirements.)	*Internal* The control of the form and content of examinations rests with the institution itself. The institution also determines performance standards and awards certificates, etc.	The institution enjoys unrestricted freedom and the autonomy to reach decisions about all aspects of the curriculum.

are typical examples of examinations that, in terms of content and structure, are controlled by schools, though within the general framework determined by the appropriate examination board. It should be noted that cases where both the examination requirements and the examinations themselves are internally controlled by a school are relatively rare and restricted to courses and programmes for which no external examinations are available.[7] Outside the school system, however, they occur more frequently. For example, most university examinations fall within this category.

The effect of our external examination structure on the curriculum manifests itself in two respects:

i The content and orientation of the curriculum in the various subject areas taught.
ii The teaching styles and strategies adopted by teachers.

These points are briefly discussed in the following section.

Influence of Examinations on the Content and Orientation of the Curriculum

In a recent publication about curriculum renewal in the sciences, Waring comments:

examination requirements . . . exert a considerable influence upon the subjects offered and taken up by pupils in schools. In the second place, their syllabuses and question papers . . . determine not only content, but also and to an ever more apparent extent, the method of teaching used.[8]

In order to understand this assertion, one has to be aware of the fact that, traditionally, GCE examinations and their predecessors have had two different functions: they serve as school-leaving examinations as well as university entrance examinations. In view of the latter role, it is not surprising that these examinations should reflect, particularly at A-level, the conceptions and perspectives of the various subjects, as they prevail at the highest levels of learning, viz. the universities. This means that the majority of GCE A-level syllabuses and related examinations follow fairly narrow academic lines. As Becher and Maclure aptly pointed out:

The secondary curriculum can be seen as a territory carved up and Balkanized into a series of separate empires over which the more powerful disciplines held sway. Operating mainly from a series of bases within higher education, they seek to colonize and inculcate the secondary schools with their values and their forms of thought . . . .'[9]

The dominant influence of the universities on the content of the secondary school courses is particularly noticeable in the science area. Science curricula and syllabuses leading to GCE A-level examinations are usually strongly oriented towards the 'pure' science side. By comparison, the applied, technological and social aspects of the sciences tend to be neglected.

The situation is similar for GCE O-level and CSE courses in that many of these simply reflect the broad orientations that are found at the higher level of secondary education. Evidence for this is found in a major report on *Aspects of Secondary Education in England* prepared by HM Inspectors of Schools in 1979.[10] In this report, the inspectors stress the importance of pupils gaining an adequate knowledge and experience of the application of scientific concepts and principles in everyday life and in the industrial and biological environment. But they also conclude, on the basis of their investigations, that in most school science courses these aspects are totally neglected. When asked about this, teachers generally asserted that the teaching demands laid down in the various examination syllabuses did not allow scope for the treatment of these themes.

In the context of a major study into the conduct of practical work as a component of school science courses Kerr, too, demonstrated the strong influence of external examination requirements on educational practice.[11] He found that teachers saw the practical activities that they arranged for their pupils chiefly as a preparation for their practical examinations, rather than as an integral part of their science education. Kerr proposed the introduction of teacher assessment of practical work as a means of counteracting the undue influence of the external examination requirements. Some of the GCE examination boards followed this proposal in the 1970s. There is some evidence to show that, as a result, the range and scope of practical work in A-level science courses has improved.[12]

Effect of Examination Requirements on Teaching Procedures

The effect of external examinations on the styles and methods of teaching is no less significant than their influence on the content of courses. Mathews had already pointed to examination syllabuses and examination papers as a major influence on a teacher's decision on 'what to teach and the manner in which it is to be taught'.[13] He also observed that the extent to which examinations exert pressure upon schools and teachers depends on the 'social and educational climate of each country' and on 'the degree to which examination results are used for selection procedures' and suggested that in England this pressure is particularly high.

Tangible evidence of the effect of examinations on teaching styles and strategies is not easy to obtain. Teachers themselves generally deny that they are unduly influenced in their teaching by examination requirements, either because they fail to recognise this influence or because they feel reluctant to admit to such influence. The HM Inspectorate survey[14] mentioned above presents at least some indications of the impact of examinations on the practice of science education. For example, the school inspectors report that

The importance of public examinations was evident in all schools, both for the individual pupils and departments. Examination success was eagerly sought by a high proportion of both pupils and teachers, but in a considerable number of schools this aim was regarded by teachers as being incompatible with a teaching style which sought to develop analytical and predictive thinking.

and

regrettably, not all the teaching methods were effective. In about one-third of the schools the teaching of science was always or nearly always overdirected, with insufficient pupil activity. Similarly, dictated or copied notes were prevalent in about half the schools. Some schools achieved good external examination results by these methods but nevertheless it was felt that the excessive use of them detracted from the overall quality of the science lessons.

Elsewhere, the report acknowledges that in some schools good teaching was observed, but proceeds to state that

unfortunately, practical work often did not go further than this [= providing skill training] and few opportunities were provided for pupils to conduct challenging experimental investigations. This is perhaps partly because some science examination syllabuses do not appear to encourage this kind of work . . . .

Such evidence as exists concerning the impact of examination demands on the nature of science teaching cannot of course be quantified, basically because it is largely impossible to devise and implement science education programmes that are not subject to at least some examination pressures. A number of the Mode 3 CSE syllabuses developed by individual schools, usually for their less able pupils, come closest to a situation where no external examination requirements have to be observed: such courses are internally examined and have often been devised by teachers with much imagination and creative thought. No doubt, this in itself contains a valuable lesson.

It is unlikely that, for as long as an external examination structure operates, the effects of such examinations on the practice of education can ever be eliminated. The task, therefore, is to channel this influence in such a way that it becomes a positive, rather than a negative one. This means that the structure and content of examinations should be so devised that they are supportive of the aims and intentions of the educational programme, instead of conflicting with them. In other words, examinations should be curriculum-led, instead of the curriculum being led by examination requirements.

An essential prerequisite for this is the clear definition and articulation of the educational aims and objectives of a course or curriculum on which the assessments and examinations are to focus. Such aims and objectives, in as much as they are appropriate for science education, are discussed in the next section.

Aims, Goals and Objectives of School Science Education

As has already been observed, in the strictest sense examinations and assessments should seek to measure the particular qualities that a curriculum or course seeks to foster in students. In the context of science education, such qualities may be divided into three broad categories:

i *Intellectual abilities and skills* that include the student's ability to recall, apply and evaluate scientific information, and to plan and devise experimental investigations, for example for the solution of scientific problems. Frequently, abilities of this nature are referred to as *cognitive* abilities.

ii *Manipulative skills and abilities* that include skills in the handling and manipulation of materials and apparatus in the context of scientific investigations, as well as the ability to follow instructions and to make accurate observations. Generally, these and related skills are referred to as *psychomotor* skills.

iii Qualities that concern students' *attitudes* towards and *interests* in science and the study of science, and science-related beliefs and values, as well as to ethical judgements and interpersonal relationships. Qualities of this nature are generally referred to as *affective* characteristics.

The foregoing classification is due to Bloom and coworkers, who have also developed detailed taxonomies for the cognitive and the affective domain of educational objectives.[15, 16] Some detailed comments concerning Bloom's taxonomy of educational objectives for the cognitive domain are given in Chapter 4.

Statements found in the literature about the qualities to be developed in students as a result of their involvement in, and exposure to, science education activities vary greatly in the precision with which these qualities are specified and the degree of behaviourism that is associated with such specifications. At the one extreme, we find statements that reflect broad philosophical or educational beliefs or values: for example, this is true for the demand that the purpose of science education should be the development of 'scientific literacy'. Statements of this type are generally referred to as *aims*. It is immediately clear that this particular statement, though sound and thoroughly justified, has little operational value (descriptively or prescriptively) in relation to curriculum planning or the design of examinations. This applies to curricular aims generally.

At the other end of the spectrum, we find statements such as 'the student should be able to describe the principal sources of hydrocarbons and the problems inherent in their characterisation'. These define a learning outcome in a very specific, though narrow sense and can immediately be translated into appropriate assessment situations. Generally, statements of this type are referred to as *objectives*.

Intermediate between these two types of statement are those that point towards a generalised behavioural outcome that is expected of the learner without, however, expressing precise performance features. The following statement from the Schools Council Integrated Science Project (SCISP) exemplifies this:

Pupils should be able to demonstrate their degree of competence in . . . organizing and formulating ideas in order to communicate them to others.[17]

Statements of this intermediate nature are sometimes referred to as *goals*, although the term 'general objective' has also been advocated to describe them. The essential characteristic of goals is that, unlike aims, they already contain an element of operationality in that they point to some ability or skill that the learner is to develop. However, such skill or ability descriptions normally require further elaboration and definition before statements emerge that can immediately be translated into suitable assessment tasks.

A distinction has to be made at this juncture between statements of educational intent that focus primarily on the learning outcomes to be achieved by the student and those that are directed chiefly at the teacher as curriculum implementor or course designer. This distinction is strongly reflected in the recent 16+ National Criteria for Science and a range of science subjects developed by the GCE and CSE Boards' Joint Council for 16+ National Criteria[18]. For example, the Science document states:

The aims [set out in the document] describe the educational purposes of a course in Science for the GCSE examination. Some of these aims are reflected in the assessment objectives; other are not because they cannot readily be translated into objectives that can be assessed. All syllabuses in GCSE Science must be constructed to enable, and should be designed to encourage, schools and colleges to provide courses which will seek to achieve these aims.

Implicit in this quotation is a further distinction, viz. between 'assessment objectives' and 'non-assessed objectives'. It should be noted that, insofar as this distinction is made, it is done for reasons of convenience and expediency: we find it difficult at times to formulate educational intentions with sufficient precision and specificity that they become measurable qualities. This is particularly true for the formulation of affective characteristics to be developed by the learner.

Tables 1.2 and 1.3 summarise the aims and the assessment objectives that have recently been accepted by the Secondary Examinations Coun-

Table 1.2. Educational aims proposed for GCSE science courses

The aims of any science education programme should be as follows:

1 To provide, through well-designed studies of experimental and practical science, a worthwhile educational experience for all pupils whether or not they go on to study science beyond this level and, in particular, to enable them to acquire sufficient understanding and knowledge:
   (a) to become confident citizens in a technological world, able to take or develop an informed interest in matters of scientific import;
   (b) to recognise the usefulness, and limitations, of scientific method and appreciate its applicability in other disciplines and in everyday life;
   (c) to be suitably prepared for studies beyond the GCSE level in pure sciences, in applied sciences or in science-dependent vocational courses.

2 To develop abilities and skills that:
   (a) are relevant to the study and practice of science;
   (b) are useful in everyday life;
   (c) encourage safe practice.

3 To stimulate:
   (a) curiosity, interest and enjoyment in science and its methods of enquiry;
   (b) interest in, and care for, the environment.

4 To promote an awareness that:
   (a) the study and practice of science are cooperative and cumulative activities and are subject to social, economic, technological, ethical and cultural influences and limitations;
   (b) the applications of sciences may be both beneficial and detrimental to the individual, the community and the environment.

Source: cf. DES GCSE *(General Certificate of Secondary Education)* – *The National Criteria (Science)* HMSO (London) 1985.

cil[19] as the binding guidelines for syllabus and curriculum development work in science and the separate science subjects. They represent an up-to-date specification of the main intentions and purposes that are associated with contemporary science education. Although they are strictly applicable only to GCSE science education programmes (for the 11 to 16 age group), the nature of these aims and objectives is such that they can broadly be applied to, for example, GCE A-level courses also.

The statements of objectives in Table 1.3 merit particular attention, for three reasons. First, it is noteworthy that practically all the objectives listed in Section 2 of the table express skills and abilities that relate to the *processes* of science, i.e. the procedures whereby scientific information and data are obtained, recorded and interpreted. Objectives dealing with the factual and conceptual content of science are relatively rare, in com-

Table 1.3. Assessment objectives proposed for GCSE science courses

Within the framework of content specified by a given syllabus, candidates are expected to demonstrate (at the end of this course):

1 Knowledge and understanding of:
  (a) scientific phenomena, facts, laws, definitions, concepts, theories;
  (b) scientific vocabulary, terminology, conventions;
  (c) scientific instruments and apparatus, including techniques of operation and aspects of safety;
  (d) scientific quantities and their determination;
  (e) scientific and technological applications with their social, economic and environmental implications.

2 Skills and abilities to:
  (a) observe, measure and record accurately and systematically;
  (b) follow instructions accurately for the safe conduct of experiments;
  (c) communicate scientific observations, ideas and arguments logically, concisely and in various forms;
  (d) translate information from one form to another;
  (e) extract from available information data relevant to a particular context;
  (f) use experimental data, recognise patterns in such data, form hypotheses and deduce relationships;
  (g) draw conclusions from, and evaluate critically, experimental observations and other data;
  (h) recognise and explain variability and unreliability in experimental measurements;
  (i) devise and carry out experimental or other tests to check the validity of data, conclusions and generalisations;
  (j) devise and carry out experiments or other tests for particular purposes, selecting suitable apparatus and using it effectively and safely;
  (k) explain familiar facts, observations and phenomena in terms of scientific laws, theories and models;
  (l) suggest scientific explanations of unfamiliar facts, observations and phenomena;
  (m) apply scientific ideas and methods to solve qualitative and quantitative problems;
  (n) make decisions based on the examination of evidence and arguments;
  (o) recognise that the study and practice of science are subject to various limitations and uncertainties;
  (p) explain technological applications of science and evaluate associated social, economic and environmental implications.

Source: cf. DES GCSE *(General Certificate of Secondary Education)* – *The National Criteria (Science)* HMSO (London) 1985.

parison with process objectives, and are contained within Section 1 of the table.

Secondly, although all the objectives point clearly towards observable (and, hence, assessable) learning outcomes to be achieved by the student, they would normally require further amplification and elaboration, e.g. in terms of the specific subject matter to which they refer, before they can be translated into assessment items. This gives them the characteristics of goals, as defined earlier on, rather than those of specific objectives. However, for as long as there exists reasonable clarity about the content to be covered in a science programme, this elaboration seldom causes major problems.

Thirdly, an inspection of the objectives reveals that they tend to express either cognitive or psychomotor qualities that the learner is expected to develop. This is in stark contrast to many of the aims statements, which point towards affective qualities. The fact that none of the latter has been transformed into objectives statements may be taken as a sign of the difficulties associated with the assessment of affective qualities.

The emphasis given in the list of assessment objectives to process skills is very much in keeping with contemporary thinking about the purposes and direction of science education. For example, the 1985 Policy Statement on science education issued by the DES contains the following statement:

[The Secretaries of State] believe that examinations should place greater emphasis than has hitherto been the case upon scientific method. Syllabuses should not be overloaded with factual content; the content which is included should be readily usable as a vehicle for developing the intellectual and practical skills of science, and it should be so used by teachers.[20]

The Assessment of Performance Unit (APU), in its science monitoring exercise, has likewise focused predominantly on science process skills and identified six broad categories:[21]

  i Dealing with symbolic representations.
  ii Use of apparatus and measuring instruments.
  iii Observation.
  iv Interpretation and application (of scientific concepts).
  v Planning investigations.
  vi Performance of investigations.

Such emphasis on science process skills is clearly warranted if one remembers that, formerly, science education was strongly oriented towards the content aspects of science and tended to pay little attention to the processes and procedures of science. Nevertheless, the issue of processes versus concepts in science has to be approached with some caution, for a number of reasons. For example, 'science' cannot merely be seen in terms of the processes with which we assume it to be associated. Science, in its totality and through its constituent branches, is concerned with a wide range of 'knowledge items' (facts, theories, rules, concepts, etc.) that is no less important a part of science than are science processes. Moreover, it is by no means established or self-evident that science can claim 'propriety rights' over the processes that are normally associated with scientific method: many other subjects, including those represented in the school curriculum, claim precisely the same processes for themselves.

Thus, science cannot be seen without linking the processes of science to the particular areas of concern and subject matter of science. It is important to bear this in mind in the interpretation of objectives such as those given in Table 1.3. Normally, it is through syllabuses or similar documents that our attention is drawn to the 'content' dimension of science or the individual sciences. It is also in relation to this content dimension that the foregoing assessment objectives have to be interpreted, not only in course development but also in the design of assessment and examination items. Only if this is done, can a sound and proper relationship between objectives and assessment be achieved.

The Science Monitoring team of APU, recognising this strong interrelationship between the process dimension and the conceptual content dimension in science, developed lists of science concepts and knowledge that it expects students to have acquired at different ages. Table 1.4 presents examples of such concepts and knowledge items used at age 15, for several broad content areas. For full information, the original APU science publications should be consulted.[22]

Issues for Consideration

The purpose of this chapter has been to identify the various functions of assessments and examinations and to point to the contexts in which they occur. Although not specifically referred to here, there are issues and problems associated with assessments and examinations. Among these are:

- the criteria by which the quality of assessment and examination procedures can be judged;
- the procedures whereby cognitive, psychomotor and affective characteristics can be estimated or determined;
- the use of profiles as a means of communicating assessment and examination results; and
- the adoption of criterion-referenced assessment procedures and potential problems associated with this development.

These and other issues will be considered in some detail in the following chapters.

Table 1.4. Examples of concept and knowledge items chosen for the APU science monitoring at age 15. (The numbering refers to the original APU listing)

A. INTERACTION OF LIVING THINGS WITH THEIR ENVIRONMENT

A1. *Interdependence of living things*

Virtually all organisms are dependent on the presence and activities of other organisms for their survival.

Green plants use energy from the sun to make food by 'photosynthesis'. During this process plants produce oxygen. Plants and animals use oxygen in respiration.

Some animals eat plants and some eat other animals, but all animals ultimately depend on green plants for food. This relationship can be illustrated by a 'food web'.

Any alteration in one part of the 'food web' may affect many other parts of the 'food web'.

An alteration in the 'food web' can be as a result of a change of balance between 'consumers' and 'producers', or of a change in the inorganic environment.

Organisms live in 'communities' in which each organism has a place in which it is best adapted to survive.

Competition and predation tend to maintain the balance of populations within a 'community'.

D. TRANSFER OF ENERGY

D1. *Work and energy*

There is a variety of sources of energy such as fuels (including food), other chemicals, deformed springs, capacitors and objects at a height.

Energy can be changed from one form to another but can never be created or destroyed. At each change some energy becomes less available for doing useful work.

Moving objects have energy which is transferred when they are stopped.

An object increases its 'potential energy' when it is raised from its original position to a greater height above the Earth's surface.

Work is done (energy is transferred) when a force moves its point of application; work is measured by the product of the force and the distance moved in the direction of the force.

The hotter the substance is, the more energy its particles have.

Different substances conduct heat at different rates. Conduction of heat can be explained in terms of the kinetic theory of matter.

The expansion of material on heating can be explained in terms of the additional energy of motion of its particles.

F. CHEMICAL INTERACTIONS

F4. *Some chemical reactions*

On heating, some compounds change colour due to loss of water. Often these changes are easily reversed.

When elements react with oxygen only, they usually form oxides; this is an example of an oxidation reaction.

When a compound changes by losing oxygen, this is an example of a reduction reaction.

The oxidation of a metal by atmospheric oxygen is an example of corrosion.

Fuels such as coal and oil are formed by the gradual decay of plant remains under high pressure.

Large amounts of energy can be transferred from these fuels when they react with oxygen. This is an example of a combustion reaction.

When an acid reacts with an alkali or a base, a salt and water are formed.

When an acid reacts with some other substances, e.g. with metals or carbonates, a salt and a gas are formed.

The process of electrolysis involves 'electron transfer' reactions which are used extensively in industry.

Source: cf. DES *Science in Schools Age 15: Report No. 4* Department of Education and Science/HMSO (London) 1985.

Notes and References

1 *Report and Papers on the Reorganisation of the Permanent Civil Service*, published as a Parliamentary report in 1854–55. The main report, by Sir Stafford H. Northcote and Sir Charles E. Trevelyan, was prepared in 1853 and proposed a Central Board of Examiners to conduct competitive examinations and the abolition of 'nomination and patronage'.

2 Taunton Commission (Schools Inquiry Commission) *Report of the Commissioners 1868*.

3 D. Lawton *Politics of the School Curriculum* Routledge and Kegan Paul (London) 1980.

4 D.L. Nuttall 'Examinations in education' in P.R. Cox, H.B. Miles and J. Peel (editors) *Equalities and Inequalities in Education* Academic Press (London) 1975 pages 67–77.

5 Waddell Committee Report *School Examinations: Report of the Steering Committee Established to Consider Proposals for Replacing the GCE 'O' level and CSE examinations by a Common System of Examining* Department of Education and Science (London) 1978.

6 DES *GCSE (General Certificate of Secondary Education) – The National Criteria* HMSO (London) 1985.

7 Mode 3 examinations that are available within the framework of the current CSE examination structure come close to this specification. For these examinations, schools develop their own syllabuses and are also responsible for the examinations relating to them. However, these activities are supervised by the appropriate CSE Board.

8 M. Waring *Social Pressure and Curriculum Innovation – A Study of the Nuffield Foundation Science Teaching Project* Methuen (London) 1979 page 10.

9 T. Becher and S. Maclure *The Politics of Curriculum Change* Hutchinson (London) 1978 page 97.

10 Department of Education and Science (DES) *Aspects of Secondary Education in England: A Survey by H.M. Inspectors of Schools* HMSO (London) 1979.

11 J.F. Kerr *Practical Work in School Science* Leicester University Press (Leicester) 1964.

12 Compare R.F. Kempa 'Teacher assessment of practical skills in chemistry' in D.E. Hoare, R.F. Kempa and P.A. Ongley *Research in Assessment II* The Chemical Society [now Royal Society of Chemistry] Assessment Group (London) 1979 pages 15–26.

13 J.C. Mathews The Effect of Examinations in Determining the Chemistry Curriculum up to the Level of University Entrance. Report prepared for the International Union of Pure and Applied Chemistry. *Pure and Applied Chemistry*, Volume II (1965), Nos. 3–4.

14 DES *Aspects of Secondary Education in England*, see note 10 above.

15 B.S. Bloom (editor) *Taxonomy of Educational Objectives: Handbook 1, Cognitive Domain* Longmans (London and New York) 1956.

16 D.R. Krathwohl (editor) *Taxonomy of Educational Objectives: Handbook 2, Affective Domain* Longmans (London) 1964.

17 Schools Council Integrated Science Project *Patterns* Longman and Penguin Books (London) 1973.

18 DES *GCSE (General Certificate of Secondary Education)*, see note 6 above.

19 The Secondary Examinations Council, together with the School Curriculum Development Committee, was established in 1982 by the Secretary of State for Education and Science, in place of the old Schools Council. Its broad function is to monitor all examination courses offered in secondary schools in England and Wales, including those administered at 18+ by the GCE Boards.

20 DES *Science 5–16: A Statement of Policy* HMSO (London) 1985.

21 DES *The Assessment Framework for Science at Ages 13 and 15 APU Science Report for Teachers No. 2* Department of Education and Science (London) 1984.

22 For science concepts at age 15, see DES *Science in Schools. Age 15: Report no. 1* HMSO (London) 1982.
A list of science concepts relevant to age 11 is given in DES *Science Assessment Framework at Age 11. APU Science Report for Teachers: No. 4* Department of Education and Science (London) 1984.

2

Review of Assessment Techniques

In science education, as well as in other branches of education, numerous different assessment methods and techniques are currently in use or have been considered for use at some stage. These range from traditional essay-type examinations at one extreme of the spectrum to oral examinations at the other. In the main, the assessment procedures currently in use aim at measuring students' achievement or performance in the cognitive domain, i.e. they measure diverse intellectual qualities such as the recall of knowledge, understanding, the ability to apply knowledge to solve problems, etc. It is true that other assessment and examination procedures are concerned with the assessment of students' 'practical skills' in science, but these have at least so far tended to be specific to particular areas of science and the skills associated with them. Therefore, it is difficult to make generalised statements concerning these techniques. Chapter 5 will consider the issues of assessing practical skills in science in some detail.

The purpose of this chapter is to present a concise overview of the customary examination and assessment procedures as they are currently used in science education, and to describe their main characteristics. The latter includes an analysis of the strengths and weaknesses, respectively, of the different assessment techniques. This, it is hoped, will be of help to science teachers in choosing the assessment procedures suitable for particular purposes.

A Classification of Assessment Techniques

For the purpose of this review, a classification system is adopted which considers the type of assessment activity or task in relation to the context in which the assessment or examination arises. In principle, two possibilities exist:

I The assessment is based on the evaluation of students' performances on tasks or assignments that are specifically designed for the purpose of assessment.

II The assessment is based on an evaluation of students' performance on tasks or assignments that are primarily planned as an integral part of a learning experience.

The distinction made here between the two types of assessment is not just one of convenience, but concerns the nature and quality of the information that may be derived from them.

When Type I assessments are conducted, the assumption is usually made that the student has completed the learning experience to which the assessment relates. Thus, the assessment will constitute a test of how well, or otherwise, the students have learned from the course or a particular course component and of the skills and competences they have acquired. In brief, Type I assessments generally establish students' *terminal* achievements.

By contrast, assessment Type II cannot establish terminal achievement in that it relates to activities or assignments that are themselves part of a student's learning programme. Its main function is normally to assess the student's progress in a course of study or to monitor work input or learning difficulties, etc. Type II assessments are basically *in-course assessments* and are conducted whilst a course is still in progress. Consequently, the results of this type of assessment cannot be taken to represent a student's terminal skills and abilities.

A particular area of science education where the distinction between the two assessment types is of significance is that of the assessment of students' practical skills and abilities. As is more fully discussed in Chapter 5, since the late 1960s and early 1970s in A-level science examinations, there has been a steady trend away from formal (three-hour) 'practical examinations' to the school- or teacher-based assessment of students' practical skills and abilities. Unlike the former, which invariably take place at the end of students' A-level courses, the teacher-based assessment mode requires students' practical skills to be assessed at regular intervals during their course of study, i.e. whilst these skills are still developing. Hence, the teacher-based assessment mode can, by definition, not lead to information about students' terminal skills in practical work in science subjects. In principle, this must raise the issue of whether it is legitimate to combine the results of such teacher-based assessments (which are of Type II described above) with the results of the Type I assessment procedures used for the major part of A-level science examinations. In practice, the assumption is made that the grades derived from teacher assessments are sufficiently indicative of students' terminal achievement in practical science that the combination of the two assessment results is justified.

For Type I assessments, the following procedures are usually employed:

i Written examinations or tests in their different forms:
 these include essay-type, short-answer and structured questions, multiple-choice tests, open-book examinations, etc.
ii Practical examinations or tests.

iii Special 'assessment' projects, etc.
iv Oral examinations and formal interviews.

Of these procedures, written examinations enjoy general popularity and acceptance, whilst the procedures given under iii and iv tend not to be used. This is largely the consequence of the pronounced role that external examinations have in British education, and that requires assessment procedures to be adopted which are easy to administer and allow students' grades to be determined with a high degree of objectivity. In the context of science education, as well as in other contexts, written examinations generally fulfil this requirement.

Type II assessments are made in relation to work undertaken by students in the course of their normal educational programme. The nature of such work varies from subject to subject, but may include the following:

v Normal laboratory work or field work.
vi Problems to be worked out or solved.
vii Projects and investigations, undertaken by students individually or in groups.

If these or similar activities are chosen as a basis for assessment, it is important to recognise that no judgement about students' terminal abilities can be made from them, for the reason stated above.

Strengths and Weaknesses of Different Assessment Procedures

It is self-evident that the various assessment procedures that are available to the teacher and examiner differ in the strengths and weaknesses associated with them, as well as in the advantages and disadvantages that they offer. Since, in an informed choice of assessment methods, their particular qualities ought to be taken into consideration, a brief analysis is presented here of the strengths and weaknesses of the main assessment procedures.

For the purpose of this analysis, the following three broad questions will be considered:

i What abilities and skills can readily be tested by the given procedure?
ii How objective, reliable and interpretable are the results derived from the particular procedures?
iii What are the problems associated with the development of tests and/or their administration?

Table 2.1 presents a summary analysis in terms of the foregoing points of the three main approaches currently in use for the assessment of cognitive abilities and skills. These are multiple-choice tests, short-answer and structured questions, and 'free-response questions', which

Table 2.1. Analysis of common procedures for the assessment of cognitive abilities and skills

Assessment method	Abilities/skills readily tested by assessment procedure, incl. abilities/ skills not easily tested
Multiple-choice/objective-type tests Note: These can include different types of item, e.g. multiple-choice items; multiple-completion items; true–false items; assertion–reason items.[a]	Particularly suitable for testing a wide range of knowledge and comprehension tasks. Higher level abilities (reasoning and problem-solving) can also be assessed adequately, provided that relevant items can be responded to in a relatively short period of time. Since answers have to be chosen from a predetermined range of responses, multiple-choice items cannot be used to test students' communication (self-expressive) skills or their ability to *formulate* answers and responses.
Short-answer/structured questions Note: Short-answer questions may be set as independent test items, or appear in sets of items which are thematically related to one another. In the latter case, they are generally referred to as 'structured questions'.	Suitable for testing a wide range of knowledge, comprehension and (simple) application tasks. Unlike multiple-choice items, short-answer questions require the student to formulate a response, rather than to select from a range of possible responses. As far as the testing of higher level abilities is concerned, short-answer questions have the same limitation as multiple-choice items. In structured questions, it is possible to arrange individual short-answer question parts in order of increasing difficulty or in a hierarchical manner, presenting low level tasks first, followed by tasks testing higher order abilities. This feature is very attractive in the design of questions for a wide ability of spectrum.

[a] H.G. Macintosh and R.B. Morrison *Objective Testing* University of London Press (London) 1969.

Comments re objectivity, reliability and interpretability of assessment results	Problems associated with development and/or administration and marking of tests used in procedure
Questions can be marked with high accuracy and objectivity. However, it should be noted that the term 'objectivity' applies to the marking process only: the drafting of questions and of responses accepted as 'correct' involves subjective judgement. High question validity and test reliability can be achieved through appropriate pretesting of items. Interpretation of results in terms of students' abilities and skills is usually easy, but it must be stressed that correct answers can be due to the cues provided by question or even guessing.	The design of good multiple-choice items is time-consuming and requires considerable 'item-writing' skills. However, once developed, items can be reused. The administration of multiple-choice tests is simple, as is their marking. For large-scale testing, machine-marking is possible.
Short answers can usually be marked with a fair degree of accuracy and, in case of multiple marking, good intermarker reliability. Decisions about what counts as 'correct answers' involve some subjectivity. Short-answer questions cannot be answered on the basis of cues (unlike multiple-choice questions) or by guessing. The interpretation of test results is usually straightforward and allows judgements to be made about strengths and weaknesses in a student's performance.	Development of a short-answer question is significantly easier than that of a multiple-choice item, since no response to the question need be considered. Short-answer questions can be marked with relative ease, but require 'hand-marking', i.e. no machine-marking is possible. This is a draw-back in large-scale test administrations.

Table 2.1. Analysis of common procedures for the assessment of cognitive abilities and skills (continued)

Essay questions/problem-solving questions

Can be used for assessing all cognitive abilities, including higher level skills. The particular strength of essay questions lies in their capacity to examine sophisticated skills, including problem-solving of a more extensive nature and synthesis tasks in the Bloomian sense (cf. Chapter 4).

Since essay-type questions usually ask for extensive answers to be given, they require students to demonstrate communicative skills and to organise their ideas.

Essay-type questions, including those testing problem-solving, tend to be significantly longer (i.e. time-consuming to answer) than multiple-choice or short-answer questions. Hence, the extent to which by means of them students' knowledge and skills can be assessed is very limited. To overcome this, a choice of questions is usually provided.

Oral examinations

In principle, this method is suitable for the assessment of all cognitive abilities and skills. Its main attraction lies in its potential for assessing higher intellectual abilities. Thus, oral techniques are frequently used in researches into problem-solving.

The interactive nature of oral examining enables the examiner to probe deeply into students' understanding and knowledge of a subject. In the course of this, areas of misunderstanding and misconceptions are likely to be revealed.

May suffer from a degree of subjectivity in marking, due often to the variety of responses to which a particular question gives rise. The reliability with which essay questions may be marked can be improved by the adoption of well-structured marking schedules. However, the drafting of such schedules is itself a highly subjective matter, not least in relation to the allocation of marks to various subsections of a question.

Marks derived from essay questions are difficult to interpret since most questions tend to test a variety of skills and abilities. Unless special analyses are made, it is not possible to interpret marks awarded in terms of student performances in particular ability/skills areas.

The problem of interpretability increases when a choice of questions is offered, since it is usually not possible to design questions of high comparability.

Essay questions and problem-solving questions are fairly easy to set so that a complete examination can be constructed in a relatively short period of time. By contrast, the marking of these questions is tedious and time-consuming.

There is considerable evidence to suggest that the judgements made by examiners in the marking of essay-type questions can be significantly influenced by the way in which an answer is presented. The use of marking schedules reduces the effect of this without, however, eliminating it altogether.

Techniques of oral examining are generally held to be unreliable and subjective, for a variety of reasons:
(a) It is difficult for examiners not to be influenced in their judgement by the verbal fluency and self-confidence of the student.
(b) The interactive nature of oral examinations leads to changes in questions asked, from candidate to candidate, thereby producing non-comparable results.
(c) Unless expensive audio-visual recording techniques are used, the examiner has to rely on the recall of the interview in making judgements about the student.

The interpretability of the results of oral examinations is very high, especially for diagnostic purposes.

In that techniques of oral examining usually require one-to-one situations to be established between examiner and examinee, they are costly and impracticable for 'large-scale' use, except in special circumstances.

are taken here to comprise essay questions and problem-solving questions. In addition, oral examining has also been included in the analysis, since it has a recognised place in some areas of education, e.g. foreign language work. In the context of science education, however, no use has so far been made of this technique, although its use has from time to time been advocated. Two particular reasons are usually advanced in favour of oral examinations: they contribute to a reduction in the dominance of written examinations and assessments in our education system, and they allow the assessment to be made in conditions that are far closer to real life than the usual written examinations.

In recent years, a range of additional techniques for the assessment of students' cognitive abilities and skills has been suggested and explored, mainly in the Further Education and Higher Education sectors. Usually, these techniques represent variations on established procedures for written examinations. Among them are the following:

(a) *Open-Book Examinations.* These are conducted like normal examinations in which the student is required to respond to essay or problem-solving questions, but the students are allowed access during the examination to textbooks and notes, etc. The rationale underlying open-book examinations is that they reduce the need for rote-learning and so allow the genuine testing of higher level abilities.

Actual experiences with open-book examinations have not always produced the advantage expected of them. Two reasons have been suggested for this. One is that the effective use of a textbook under examination conditions depends on a high degree of familiarity with its layout and content. The second reason is that, unless questions are skilfully designed and structured, the regurgitation of textbook material is encouraged.

(b) *Examination with 'Seen Questions' or 'Information about Questions'.* In these, the student is provided with specific information about the questions to be answered, prior to the examination. The purpose of this is to reduce the examinee's uncertainty (and hence anxiety) about what to expect in an examination and to prepare in depth for the areas to be tested in the examination. This, it is agreed, makes the examination a fairer test of ability in that the 'luck' element is largely eliminated.

The obvious disadvantage of this procedure is that it encourages the student to concentrate revision work in those areas that feature in the examination. Also, the fact that all students can prepare in advance for questions relating to specific topics or issues reduces the discrimination that is achievable between students of different ability.

Both open-book examinations and examinations involving 'seen questions' are assessment methods that are suitable only for relatively sophisticated students. They must thus be judged unsuitable for most, if not all, assessment tasks that arise in the context of school science education. Even if this were not the case, it is unlikely that these two approaches would find ready acceptance. Both teachers and taught tend to operate and accept only those assessment procedures that reflect those used by examining boards.

To return to Table 2.1, the three modes of written examinations listed there are now used by all GCE and CSE Boards for their written science examinations. It is evident from the analysis presented in the table that the various question types differ as regards their suitability for testing particular abilities. Therefore, the use of all three modes allows examiners to design well-balanced examinations by means of which all desired abilities or skills can be adequately tested.

Examination and Assessment Specifications

Because of their brevity and precise nature, multiple-choice and short-answer questions can readily be analysed and classified in terms of both the particular abilities tested by them and the subject matter (or syllabus sections) to which they relate. In assigning these questions to ability and/or syllabus content categories, it is necessary to bear in mind the background of the population to be examined. In the majority of cases, this presents no problem, since it is relatively easy to distinguish between test items appropriate for A-level and for O-level GCE or CSE students, respectively.

Items developed for incorporation into operational GCE and CSE examinations are now categorised according to subject matter and abilities tested, as a matter of course. As a result, all examining boards have established major item banks, mainly for multiple-choice questions. These usually contain several hundred different test items, each carefully classified, and new items are regularly added to existing ones, thus enlarging the item bank. Thus, item banks constitute a 'reservoir' of questions on which examiners can draw in the design of examination papers.

It is now standard practice for operational multiple-choice examination papers to be set in accordance with test specifications laid down in, for example, syllabuses and course guides. In a number of instances, this practice has been extended to short-answer question papers also, and there is no reason why this should not become the norm.

Several examining boards have adopted a 'grid system' in order to represent the specification agreed for particular examination papers. Figure 2.1 shows an example of a grid specification. It is based on the specification for the multiple-choice objective test (Paper 2) of the GCE O-level Chemistry examination of the University of London School Examination and University Entrance Department.

As may be seen, the grid specifies the approximate percentage weightings to be given in the multiple-choice paper to four 'ability' areas and six different 'activity' areas. The former are based on the Bloomian

Fig. 2.1 Example of a test specification grid for O-level Chemistry.

Abilities	Main study area (Activities)						Approximate percentage of marks
	Composition of materials and chemical changes	Patterns of chemical behaviour	Chemical concepts and principles	Experimental techniques and design of experiments	Quantitative aspects of chemistry, incl. calculations	Chemistry in Society	
1. Knowledge – the ability to recall information and data							40
2. Comprehension – the ability to translate and interpret information							30
3. Application – the ability to apply knowledge to new situations, especially for problem-solving							20
4. Analysis/Evaluation – the ability to analyse and evaluate information and data							10
Approximate percentage of marks	25	20	20	10	15	10	100

taxonomy (cf. Chapter 4), whilst the latter indicate the main conceptual areas in which the students are expected to develop competences and skills. Instead of stating percentage weightings, it is also possible to specify the approximate number of test items for each ability and activity area that is to appear in each operational examination paper.

The reference to activity areas, in the design of test specification grids, has proved to be particularly useful and convenient for chemistry. The reason for this is that the content and processes covered in most chemistry courses can fairly readily be analysed and organised in terms of such activities. For other subjects, unifying concepts corresponding to the chemist's activities are more difficult to define and identify. When this is the case, it is simpler to analyse the content of an examination paper in terms of syllabus sections rather than of activities. This is the case in, for example, the test specification grid for the London Board's O-level Physics examination.

From a theoretical point of view, it may be argued that a complete specification of an examination or assessment schedule should consider three aspects:

i   The range of abilities/skills to be tested.
ii The activities with respect to which such abilities/skills are to be demonstrated.
iii The subject matter areas to which the various activities relate.

If all these aspects were considered, a three-dimensional specification grid would have to be drawn up. Although for an examination consisting of a range of separate papers, such an elaborate specification might be of some value, for a single paper it is too elaborate to be operationally meaningful. Consider, for example, a situation in which an examination were to relate to four ability levels, six activity areas and six syllabus (or subject matter) sections. For each combination of ability, activity and syllabus section to be covered, a minimum of $4 \times 6 \times 6 = 144$ individual items would be required. This is clearly impossible to achieve in a single paper, even if it is of the multiple-choice type (normally, the maximum number of items incorporated into a multiple-choice paper is 70, with 50 items per test being the 'norm'). Consequently, test specifications for single papers tend to be two-dimensional, specifying abilities to be tested and either activity or syllabus (subject matter) sections.

Assessment and test specifications of the type indicated make it possible to set and compile examinations and tests in such a way that they reflect accurately the abilities, activities and subject areas to be tested and the weighting to be given to each. The advantages of this are particularly evident when examinations testing the same course or curriculum have to be set on a regular, recurrent basis, as is the case for most public examinations. Without doubt, the extensive use of fairly precise test specifications by GCE and CSE Boards has done much to improve both the validity and comparability of the objective type examination papers (multiple-choice, short- and structured answer) set by them. As a result, these papers have become very sophisticated and dependable instruments for the assessment of students' cognitive skills.

Some Problems Concerning Essay-type Questions

As is indicated in Table 2.1, traditional essay-type questions suffer from several disadvantages that limit their suitability as reliable assessment instruments. Among them are the relatively high subjectivity in the marking of answers to essay-type questions, the difficulty in interpreting meaningfully the marks or grades derived from them, and not least the lack of comparability between different, seemingly equivalent, questions set in the same paper.

Despite their obvious shortcomings, essay-type questions continue to be used in many science examinations, although the total weighting given to them may be relatively low. In typical GCE A-level examinations, the proportion of total marks allocated to 'open-ended' (essay-type and problem-solving), as opposed to objective-type questions, is generally not higher than one-third.

The main arguments for the retention in most public examinations of at least some 'open-ended' element are these:

i Essay-type and problem-solving questions are particularly suitable for testing students' higher level abilities, especially their ability to select relevant information and data and to organise them to arrive at a reasoned argument and judgement.

ii Since most science courses and curricula seek to develop students' communication abilities, open-ended (essay-type) questions offer the best means of testing these abilities.

Thus, assessment procedures involving essay-type and problem-solving questions can claim to have a legitimate place within the whole spectrum of techniques available for the assessment of cognitive abilities and skills. In view of this, it is appropriate to consider some of the special problems associated with them. Two such problems merit particular attention: (a) the unreliability in the marking of essay questions; and (b) the effect of question choice.

The Marking of Essay-type Questions

As long ago as 1935, Hartog and Rhodes[1] observed that the marking of essay-type questions by examiners gave rise to non-concordant results. On the basis of their findings, they claimed that different examiners are likely not only to assign different marks to the same essay marked by them but also to arrive at different rank orders for the same group of candidates assessed by them.

Although Hartog and Rhodes' study has been criticised on technical grounds,[2] such criticisms do not dispel the doubts raised by them about the reliability and objectivity with which essay-type questions can be marked. Information from research studies, about the extent to which the marking of essay-type questions is subject to unreliability, is relatively scarce and generally relates to the marking of English compositions. Thus, no direct information is available about the marking of free-response questions in science.

In the main, such studies as have been published have focused on the degree of consistency among the marks or grades awarded by different examiners for the same essays. The results of these studies are usually expressed in terms of correlation coefficients that denote the extent of agreement achieved between markers.

Correlation coefficients reported in the literature as expressing the agreement between the grades awarded by different assessors vary widely. For example, in a study of multiple marking of English compositions, an average intercorrelation of 0.51 was found among nine examiners.[3] This must be regarded as an unsatisfactorily low agreement, although – when the examiners were randomly assigned to three teams of markers whose individual grades were pooled – the interteam correlations were considerably higher than the intermarker correlations (approximately 0.80). The immediate conclusion that may be drawn from this is that marks or grades derived from the multiple marking of essays should be significantly more reliable than those obtained from a single assessment. This is a strong argument in support of the notion that essays should always be 'double-marked'.

It is generally believed that the use of 'analytic' marking procedures results in a higher intermarker consistency than does impressionistic marking. The evidence on this point is conflicting in that several studies reported in the literature failed to show up any major difference between the two methods. Therefore, the use of impressionistic marking of free-response questions in science should not be rejected, despite the fact that customarily examiners have marked such questions in accordance with detailed, analytical marking schemes. It is interesting to quote Mathews[4] in this context. Referring to the writing and marking of free-response questions in A-level Chemistry courses, he recommends *inter alia*:

i The questions should allow a genuine free response, at least in part. It is likely that he [*the examiner*] will be able to forecast a good deal of the material which will be contained in an answer; but, if he can forecast it all, he should consider changing the question.

ii If it is at all possible, double marking by impression using a six-point scale, $5 - 4 - 3 - 2 - 1 - 0$, should be adopted. It may be that the double marking will have to be done by the same teacher, but if it is possible to obtain the cooperation of colleagues in this matter, it would be very helpful in improving the grading.

The Effect of Question Choice

Unlike multiple-choice and structured response questions papers, those containing free-response (essay-type) questions usually allow students a choice of questions to be answered. Situations where, in operational examination papers, students are required to answer three out of eight or four out of ten questions are by no means rare. Were the choice of questions to be made on a purely random basis, the possible number of question combinations would be 56 and 210, respectively, for the two situations mentioned.

Although examiners will always endeavour to achieve a reasonable measure of comparability among the optional questions appearing in a free-response paper, in practice these attempts are not always successful. Willmott and Hall, in a major study into the effect of question choice on examination results, carefully scrutinised candidates' performances on essay-type questions appearing in various operational O-level papers.[5] One set of results obtained by them is summarised in Table 2.2.

It is immediately apparent from the table that the eight questions vary considerably in their difficulty. Questions 1 and 4 evidently were 'easy' ones, whilst questions 5, 6 and particularly 8 proved distinctly more difficult. The examination to which the figures refer required students to answer four questions. In order to visualise the effect of question choice

Table 2.2. Performance statistics for different essay-type questions in an operational O-level Biology examination

	Question number							
	1	2	3	4	5	6	7	8
Popularity (percentage of candidates attempting question)	63	51	52	62	44	37	47	39
Mean percentage	50.6	39.9	38.7	48.9	30.0	34.6	33.2	19.4
Standard deviation (percentage)	20.0	18.0	18.0	19.2	16.0	17.2	18.0	10.4

on examination results, assume that two candidates, each of 'average' ability, had chosen the four easiest and the four most difficult questions, respectively. This would have produced a difference of about 15% in their percentage scores, entirely as a result of question selection. Were one to assume a weighting of 40% for the essay-type paper in the overall examination, this difference would be equivalent to about 6% of the total marks.

A further interesting finding reported by Willmott and Hall is that candidates tend to answer questions in the order in which they appear on the paper, and that questions at the beginning of a paper generally enjoy greater popularity than those appearing in the second half. The popularity figures in Table 2.2 bear this out. The relative placement of questions in an examination paper must thus be seen as a further 'chance factor' influencing the mark score that a candidate can gain.

The foregoing comments point clearly to the problematic nature of the use of essay questions in operational examinations, especially if question choice is allowed. On measurement grounds alone, a strong case could be made against the continued use of optional free-response questions. However, there exists an equally strong argument in favour of their retention. This is that they are the only means whereby, in the context of written examinations, students' communicative skills and abilities can be assessed. As was seen in Chapter 1, such skills rank highly among the goals and objectives of science education. What constitutes communication skills and how they can be assessed is explored in Chapter 4.

Oral Examinations

Table 2.1 also makes brief reference to oral examining and describes its main features. Although oral examinations must be considered to be the oldest form of assessment (they were used well before formal written examinations were introduced), they have not found any real degree of acceptance outside the Higher Education sector. Even there, they tend to be used predominantly in connection with Higher Degree examining.

The arguments against the use of oral examinations in the context of secondary education are strong ones, and rest on reservations about technical matters, e.g. their reliability, as well as on reasons of practicability. It is probably true that, as Heywood has suggested,[6] the reliability of oral examining can be improved through a clarification of what such examinations are to assess and through an appropriate training of examiners. But this would not deal with the question of whether they are an effective and practicable method of assessment.

Unlike the usual written methods of assessment, oral examining is essentially interactive in that it depends on the exchange of information between examiner and examinee. It obviates the necessity for answers to be articulated in a written format and may thus be of potential value for the assessment of students who find it easier to communicate orally, rather than in writing. Certainly, interviewing procedures have already proved invaluable in diagnostic testing in science.[7] However, much development and research work still remains to be carried out in the area of oral examining before these techniques can find acceptance on a par with the established ones.

Conclusion

The purpose of this chapter has been to present a review of the main assessment techniques currently in use and to examine the advantages and disadvantages associated with them.

Teachers and examiners have now at their disposal a wide range of different methods for the assessment of students' skills and abilities, although these may vary in the precision and accuracy of the assessment results to which they give rise. It is this precision and accuracy that ultimately determine the quality of an assessment. How this quality can be judged and what factors affect it is the subject of the next chapter.

Notes and References
1 P. Hartog and E.C. Rhodes *An Examination of Examinations* Macmillan (London) 1935.
2 P.E. Vernon *The Measurement of Abilities* University of London Press (London) 1965.
3 J.M. Britton, N.C. Martin and H. Rosen *Multiple Marking of English Compositions* HMSO (London) 1966.
4 Nuffield Advanced Science *Chemistry – Examinations and Assessment* Penguin (Harmondsworth, Middlesex) 1972.
5 A.S. Willmott and C.G.W. Hall *'O' Level Examined: The Effect of Question Choice* Macmillan Education (London) 1975.
6 J. Heywood *Assessment in Higher Education* John Wiley & Sons (London) 1977.
7 R.J. Osborne and J.K. Gilbert 'A method for investigating concept understanding in science.' *European Journal of Science Education*, Volume 2 (1980) pages 311–21.

3

Some Technical Aspects of Testing and Examining

Any assessment or examination, whatever its purpose, may be thought of as an act of measurement. In the majority of instances, e.g. in achievement testing or formal examinations, we seek to arrive at fairly quantitative information about a student's knowledge of subject matter or practical skills, etc. In other instances, we may be content with information which is less quantitative and more qualitative, e.g. when judging a pupil's attitude towards a subject studied or a particular activity. But, even in the latter kind of situation, some facet of the pupil's work or behaviour will have to be observed and evaluated – so, here too, an act of measurement is involved.

This chapter deals with a number of technical issues that concern the nature and quality of measurements involved in examinations and assessments. In the first part, some general criteria are discussed by which the quality of tests and examinations procedures can be judged. Thereafter, the issue of 'standards and references' in educational measurements is considered.

Accuracy and Precision in Educational Measurements

In order to arrive at a set of criteria whereby the quality of educational measurements may be judged, we may initially consider the requirements that are usually associated with scientific measurements. Two main requirements present themselves:

  i Data derived from (scientific) measurements should be *accurate*.
 ii Such data should be *precise*.

The two terms implied here, viz. *accuracy* and *precision*, each have their own specific meaning. The first refers to the *closeness* of a scientific datum to an externally agreed or imposed standard. The second, by contrast, refers to the internal consistency of a set of data or, expressed differently, the reproducibility of the data. To exemplify this distinction, consider a series of titration results obtained in the course of a volumetric chemical analysis. The concordance of the titres is effectively a measure of the reproducibility or precision of the titration results. A set of concordant results would be regarded as precise, whilst a series of divergent results would lack precision. For a set of titres to be accurate, it is not only necessary for the titres to be concordant but the volumes recorded must also be exact in terms of the agreed unit of volume. Obviously, in the case of a titration, this would depend on the calibration of the burette.

Two points emerge from the foregoing. First, it is meaningless to attribute a high accuracy to scientific data that are not also precise. High precision must be taken as a precondition for accuracy, although this does not mean that precise data are inevitably accurate. The second point is that the notion of accuracy, when used in relation to scientific data, implies the existence of some reference or standard with respect to which the results of a measurement are expressed. Such standards invariably tend to be *external* to the system under investigation and are normally laid down by agreement within the scientific community. As will be seen later, educational measurements often differ in this respect from scientific measurements.

In the context of educational measurements, the notions that correspond roughly to accuracy and precision in scientific measurements are those of *validity* and *reliability*, respectively. According to Lindquist, the validity of a test (or an examination) may be defined

as the accuracy with which it measures that which it is intended to measure or as the degree to which it approaches infallibility in measuring what it purports to measure.[1]

This particular definition has the attraction of drawing attention to the qualities which we seek to measure in examinations and assessments, and raising the question of how useful a measuring procedure is for this purpose. In relation to an examination in which students' achievements in a course or curriculum are to be determined, the validity of the examination procedure would depend on the degree to which its content and tasks reflected the intended outcomes of the course or curriculum. Approaches by which the validity of tests and examinations may be determined are discussed below.

The concept of reliability in educational measurements corresponds closely to that of precision in the scientific context. Reliability expresses the consistency or concordance with which a set of test or examination scores measures a particular chosen quality. Implicit in this definition is the notion of multiple measurements from which the concordance of results may be deduced. In the scientific context, such multiple measurements are commonplace; in the educational context, by contrast, they are often impossible to conduct, as in the case of formal examinations, for example. However, a variety of techniques exists whereby the reliability of a test or examination may be estimated. The most common of these are described in the next section.

As far as the relation between validity and reliability in educational measurements is concerned, the same argument applies that has been advanced for the link between accuracy and precision in scientific measurements. A test or examination can be valid only to the extent to which it is reliable. However, a test that produces results of high consistency or reproducibility is not necessarily a valid one in that the qualities that it measures may be different from those that it purports to measure. Thus, reliability is a necessary, but not sufficient, condition for validity.

How can the Validity of Tests and Examinations be Assessed?

Measures of the validity of tests and examinations divide broadly into two categories:

i Procedures which involve the direct scrutiny and analysis of tests and examinations by 'expert judges' (e.g. teachers or examiners); these lead to the estimation of *direct* validity.
ii Procedures which depend upon the statistical comparison of tests and examination results with scores obtained from an independent test; these give measures of *derived* validity.

Procedures that give rise to estimates of direct validity have the advantage that they are relatively easy to carry out and do not require the availability of actual test scores and criterion scores derived from an independent test. This makes them very attractive in the initial design of tests and examinations. Once a test or examination has been drafted, it is submitted to a panel of independent judges who will scrutinise each item or question in terms of, for example, its relationship to the course content or examination objectives, etc. Items or questions that are judged not to conform to the agreed criteria, or over which the judges' opinion is divided, are considered to be invalid or of low validity and, hence, excluded from the operational form of the test or examination.

Since measures of direct validity rely extensively on the judgement of persons, they tend to be less objective than measures of derived validity. Also, whereas in the case of the latter the extent of a correspondence between two sets of examination or test can readily be expressed quantitatively (usually in the form of correlation coefficient), this is difficult to achieve meaningfully for measures of direct validity. The reason for this is that the number of expert judges whom one can call upon in a validation exercise is usually too small for a quantitative evaluation to be made.

Table 3.1. Types of validity and their characteristics

Type of validity	Main criterion used in its determination
Content validity (Curricular validity)	Extent to which a test or examination samples the content and/or the range of objectives of the course or curriculum to which it relates. (Direct validity measure.)
Construct validity	Degree to which a test measures the particular (psychological) qualities or traits that it purports to measure. (Derived validity measure.)
Concurrent validity	Extent to which scores derived from a test relate to scores obtained on an external criterion. (Derived validity measure.)
Predictive validity	Extent to which scores derived from a test or examination are indicative of performance at a later time. (Derived validity measure.)

Method used for its determination	Example
Examine the content of the test or examination and determine the extent to which it reflects the subject matter and objectives covered in the course or curriculum. This kind of evaluation is normally undertaken by 'expert' judges.	Assessment of a multiple-choice science test as regards 'syllabus coverage' and in terms of the abilities tested by individual items, by a moderating panel, would establish the content validity of the test.
Compare the scores derived from the test with independent measures of the qualities or traits to be measured by the test. The evaluation itself relies on statistical analysis of either correlation or concordance.	The 'construct validity' of a test designed to measure students' 'motivation in science learning' may be established by comparing test scores with science teachers' perception and ratings of the students' motivation in science lessons.
Establish the correlation between the two sets of scores. A high correlation indicates a high concurrent validity.	The 'concurrent validity' of a paper-and-pencil test for measuring pupils' practical abilities in science may be determined by comparing scores on the test with ratings of actual practical performance.
Determine the correlation between the performance scores on the earlier and later tests or examinations. If predictive use of test or examination result is intended, regression of outcome measure and test scores has to be determined.	Use of O-level examination grades in a science (or other subject) as predictors of subsequent performance at A-level. Use of A-level results, for example, for selection and placement purposes assumes high predictive validity of the former.

Table 3.1 presents in outline the main types of validity and their characteristics, together with an example of each. For a discussion of other types of validity, standard texts on educational and psychological measurement should be consulted. It may be seen from the table that the various validity measures differ with respect to the criteria employed for their determination. Thus, there exists no basis on which different validity measures can be compared with one another.

Estimating the Reliability of Tests and Examinations

The reliability of a test or an examination refers to the reproducibility of the scores derived from it for a particular group of examinees. The usual index of reliability is the *reliability coefficient*. This may be defined as the coefficient of correlation between a set of scores obtained from the examinees on the given test or examination and another set of scores obtained independently from the same examinees on an equivalent test. Two important points emerge from this definition. The first is that, although we may talk colloquially about the 'reliability of a test', reliability is the property of a test when used with a particular group of examinees. It follows from this that a test can have different reliabilities when applied to different populations. The more different these populations, the greater tends to be the divergence in the reliability coefficient.

The second point is that in terms of the above definition, the estimation of test reliability requires the results from at least two independent administrations of equivalent tests to the same population of examinees to be available. In practice, this requirement is difficult to fulfil for two reasons: (i) the preparation of equivalent forms of a test is arduous and time-consuming; and (ii) the duplicate administration of tests likewise is time-consuming but also tedious. Therefore, preference is usually given to methods for the estimation of test reliabilities that do not involve the use of multiple forms of a test and/or repeated test administration.

Table 3.2 summarises the main methods available for the estimation of test reliabilities and gives brief descriptions of their characteristics. The first two of these (the equivalent forms method and the test–retest method) are associated with several disadvantages and therefore tend not to be used in practice. Of the remaining two methods, the split-halves procedure often provides the most dependable and convenient approach to the estimation of test reliability. Unlike methods that involve the determination of the internal consistency of tests, the split-halves procedure can readily be applied to 'non-homogeneous' tests or examinations, provided that two equivalent or near-equivalent test halves can be defined. This makes it particularly suitable for the evaluation of the reliability of examination results.

The precondition for the use of internal-consistency methods for the estimation of test reliability is that tests should be fairly 'homogeneous', which means that all test items should measure the same trait or ability. Where this is not the case, the test should be treated as being composed of a number of subtests and a reliability estimate for each subtest be found. Internal-consistency methods are easiest to use with tests consisting of items that can be marked dichotomously, e.g. either as right or wrong or as true or false, etc. This makes them especially convenient for the estimation of the reliability of multiple-choice and similar tests.

Interpreting Reliability Coefficients

In order to interpret reliability coefficients, it is useful to think in terms of (hypothetical) *true scores* that could be determined by means of a test, and the actual scores obtained from it. The question that may now be posed is this: to what extent do the actual scores obtained on the test correlate with the true scores? The answer depends on the reliability of the test, as expressed by its reliability coefficient, r_{tt}. A value of $r_{tt} = 1.00$ indicates perfect agreement to exist between the two sets of scores, whereas a reliability coefficient of 0.00 would express the complete absence of any relationship between them. Intermediate positions would be represented by r_{tt} values between 0.00 and 1.00. (Negative values of r_{tt} indicate that an inverse relationship existed between the two sets of score.)

Since true scores are hypothetical in nature and not measurable in practice, the above question about the correlation between true and actual scores has only theoretical significance. However, the issue may be examined from a different point of view. Each score actually obtained may be thought of as comprising two components, the 'true' score, which would have been obtained with a perfectly reliable test, and an error component, which is due to the test unreliability:

$$S_{actual} = S_{true} + S_{error}.$$

For a set of actual scores, all of which have been obtained by means of the same test, the total (actual) variance of the scores may similarly be divided into a 'true' variance and an error variance:

$$V_{total} = V_{true} + V_{error}.$$

In this, the true variance represents that part of the total variance that would have been obtained if all measurements had been free from error. In practice, of course, every measurement is associated with errors, and thus the error variance, V_{error}, itself is never negligible. However, the amount of error variance, as part of the total variance, can vary from test

Table 3.2. Main methods for estimating test reliabilities

Method	Procedure involved in method
Equivalent forms method	Equivalent (or parallel) forms of a test or an examination are developed and administered to the same population of examinees. Correlational analysis between the sets of scores for the two forms of the test yields reliability coefficient.
Test–retest method	The same test or examination is administered to the same group of examinees on two different occasions, sufficiently separate in time to reduce the memory 'carry over' from the first to the second test administration. The reliability is found from the correlation between the two sets of scores.
Split-halves method	Only one test is administered, but divided into two 'equivalent' halves. The reliability coefficient is computed from the scores on the two halves of the test.
Internal-consistency methods	These are designed to examine the internal equivalence or consistency of items included in a test. This is derived from a statistical analysis of students' performances on each test item. Suitable procedures were developed by Kuder and Richardson[a] and by Cronbach[b].

a G.F. Kuder and M.W. Richardson 'The theory of the estimation of test reliability.' *Psychometrica*, Volume 2 (1937) pages 151–60.

b L.F. Crowbach *Essentials of Psychological Testing* Harper (New York) 1970.

Comments on method	Comments on reliability measure obtained
Parallel forms of test or examination papers are required – these are usually not available or are difficult to prepare. Duplicate testing is needed; hence the method is time-consuming.	The quality of reliability estimates obtained by this method depends primarily on the test designer's skill to produce genuinely equivalent forms of a test or examination.
Simpler than parallel forms procedure since only one test is required, but still involves duplicate testing.	Reliability estimates obtained by this method may be adversely affected by memory 'carry over' from first to second test administration (resulting in an inflated estimate) and the real changes in students' knowledge etc., in the interval between test administrations (resulting in underestimates).
Only one test and one test administration are needed. Method requires two test-halves to be formed; this can be done by 'item matching' or by separating odd- and even-numbered questions.	Provided that the two test-halves are equivalent obvious drawbacks are associated with this method. Reliability coefficients, r_h, computed from scores on the test-halves, require adjustment to give reliability coefficient, r_f, for the full-length test: $r_f = 2r_h /(1 + r_h)$
These methods are convenient to use, especially when computation facilities are available, but are applicable only to tests which are designed to be 'homogeneous' (i.e. where each item seeks to measure the same trait) and contain a large number of items.	Reliability estimates obtained from internal consistency methods are strongly affected by item characteristics, e.g. item difficulty, discriminating power and inter-item correlations. Reliability coefficients calculated for tests with considerable 'non-homogeneity' must be treated with caution.

Fig. 3.1 Graphical representation of variance partitioning for two tests of different reliability.

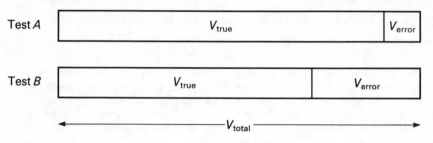

to test, as is shown in Fig. 3.1. Here, test A is assumed to have 90% 'true' variance and 10% error variance, whilst for test B the corresponding figures are 70% and 30%, respectively.

Of the two tests, the first one is clearly more reliable than the second, in that the amount of error variance associated with it is the lower of the two. Thus, it becomes possible to establish a relationship between the reliability of a test and its 'true' variance, which leads to an alternative definition of test reliability:

Reliability is the ratio of the true variance of a test to its total variance.

In simple mathematical terms, r_{tt} may be expressed in the following forms:

$$r_{tt} = V_{true}/V_{total}, \quad \text{or} \quad r_{tt} = (V_{total} - V_{error})/V_{total}.$$

The second of these formulae is of particular interest, since it relates the reliability of a test (or examination) directly to its error variance, i.e. that part of the total variance that stems from errors in the test scores. The lower this error variance, the higher is the test reliability and vice versa. Likewise, the improvement of the reliability of a test or examination depends essentially on whether its error variance can be decreased. Suggestions for achieving this are discussed in the following section.

For our next point, it is expedient to return to the definition of reliability given at the beginning of this section, according to which the reliability of a test expresses the degree of correlation between actual and 'true' scores. Assume that we had available, for a given group of students, information about their 'true' achievement grades (i.e. their 'true' scores), as well as their actual grades derived from an achievement test. What would be the agreement between the two sets of grades, for tests of different reliability? Table 3.3 illustrates the extent of agreement or disagreement, respectively, between 'true' and actual grades for three different test reliabilities, for a four-point grading system and equal

Table 3.3. Effect of test reliabilities on the predictive qualities of examinations grades. An equal distribution over four grades has been assumed. Underlined figures give percentages of accurately predicted grades

Reliability: $r_{tt}=0.80$ *Total of correct predictions: 54.3%*

Assigned grade	'True' grade (%)			
	A	B	C	D
A	<u>67.5</u>	25.3	6.6	0.6
B	25.3	<u>41.0</u>	27.1	6.6
C	6.6	27.1	<u>41.0</u>	25.3
D	0.6	6.6	25.3	<u>67.5</u>

Reliability: $r_{tt}=0.60$ *Total of correct predictions: 42.8%*

Assigned grade	'True' grade (%)			
	A	B	C	D
A	<u>53.7</u>	27.7	14.1	4.5
B	27.7	<u>31.8</u>	26.4	14.4
C	14.1	26.4	<u>31.8</u>	27.7
D	4.5	14.1	27.7	<u>53.7</u>

Reliability: $r_{tt}=0.40$ *Total of correct predictions: 35.3%*

Assigned grade	'True' grade (%)			
	A	B	C	D
A	<u>42.8</u>	27.7	19.1	10.4
B	27.7	<u>27.7</u>	25.5	19.1
C	19.1	25.5	<u>27.7</u>	27.7
D	10.4	19.1	27.7	<u>42.8</u>

grade distribution. In each set of data, the underlined figures represent the percentages of grades correctly assigned on the basis of the actual scores. For example, in the case of a test of reliability $r_{tt} = 0.80$, 67.5% of the A-grade students would actually have received an A-grade; likewise only 41.0% of the B- and C-grade students would have been assigned the correct grade. For the other test reliabilities, the corresponding figures are lower still.

The table also gives the percentages of grades that deviate from the true grade by one, two or three grade points. It is seen that, as the reliability of a test decreases, the deviations become increasingly more numerous and increase in magnitude. Thus, in the case of a test reliability of 0.80, nearly 7% of the grades awarded would differ by two or more grade points from the 'true' grades; for a test reliability of only 0.40, nearly 25% of the grades would depart by at least two points from the 'true' grades.

The extent to which agreement between actual and 'true' scores is obtained on the basis of different degrees of test reliability is also affected by the number of grade categories employed. The general rule is this: for a given test reliability (other than $r_{tt} = 1.00$), an increase in the number of grade categories leads to an increase in the proportion of wrong grade assignments. Since most school and public examinations seek to segregate pupils' performances into at least four and sometimes even seven categories (as in A-level examinations, for example), the consequences of inadequate test or examination reliabilities become self-evident.

Improving the Reliability of Tests and Examinations

It follows from the foregoing that the 'predictive' qualities of a test, in the sense that actual test scores can be used to predict 'true' scores, are strongly dependent on the reliability of the test, as well as on the number of grade categories employed. A further factor that affects the reliability and, hence, the predictive qualities of a test or examination is its length. The general rule that may be given in relation to this latter point is this: as the number of items or tasks in a test or examination is increased, its reliability increases. However, this relationship is not a linear one. Rather, it is found that the higher the reliability of a test, the smaller is the increase in this reliability that may be achieved by the lengthening of a test. More precise information about this may be obtained from the relevant literature dealing with test theory.

The main intention in this section is to consider ways of improving test reliability. The key to this is the reduction of the error variance associated with the scores derived from a test (see page 41). To do so, requires an appreciation of the various sources of error that may contribute to the errors in the scores measured by a test.

Errors associated with test scores can originate from at least three sources:

i Variations in the student that affect his or her performance on a particular task. Such variations may be due to changes in the student's alertness, motivation, speed, etc. In the case of a significant time interval between test administrations (as would occur in test–retest procedures), additional learning during the interval may be an additional factor.

ii Variations in the tasks incorporated in a test or examination or attempted by students. Although such tasks may superficially be judged to be equivalent, e.g. in terms of the abilities they measure, differences in task formulation or subject matter may affect students' performances, thus giving rise to errors.

iii Variations in the standards and objectivity applied in the marking of tests and examinations. This produces unreliability in the scores or marks awarded by the marker.

Measures to improve the reliability of tests and examinations must address themselves directly to the sources of error listed under (i) to (iii). The following are simple rules whereby this may be achieved for tests or examinations.

1 Avoid 'speeded tests' and, instead, allow adequate time for all examinees to complete the test.

2 Ensure that a test or examination contains an adequate number of items designed to measure a particular quality or trait (principle of improving reliability by lengthening of test).

3 Aim at uniformity in the presentation of test or examination questions, in preference to producing heterogeneous tests or examinations.

4 Reduce or eliminate choice of questions in examinations, and avoid ambiguity in the formulation of examination tasks.

5 Avoid 'impression' marking and, instead, employ meaningful assessment schedules for the marking of tests and examinations. (Note however, the comment about the marking of essay questions made on page 31.) Automated scoring procedures, such as those employed by examination boards for the marking of multiple-choice tests, eliminate marker unreliability altogether.

References in Educational Measurements

For the results of any measurement, educational or scientific, to be interpretable in a meaningful way requires a knowledge of the standard or 'reference' against which the measurement was carried out. In the field of science, such standards are provided by the 'units of measurement' laid down by, for example, the British Standards Institute or the *Système International d'Unités* (S.I.). Thus, for example, in determining the mass or volume of a body, we make implicit comparison with the accepted units of mass and volume, respectively, and express the results of the measurements as multiples of these units.

In the educational field, the question of the reference against which the measurement is made, or in terms of which the result of a measurement is expressed, is more complex. In principle, two different positions present themselves:

i The educational measurement is made with respect to criteria that are externally agreed and predetermined. Such criteria may express, for example, particular skills or achievement levels, etc., and can usually be derived from an analysis of the performance desired of a student at the end of a course. Measurements of this kind are said to be *criterion-referenced* and yield information that is directly interpretable in terms of specified performance standards.

ii The standard against which the educational measurement is made is not externally imposed, but derived from within the examined population. The essential feature of this is that the score of one examinee is interpreted in terms of norms obtained from the scores of the other examinees. Measurements of this kind are termed *norm-referenced*. Unlike criterion-referenced measurements, norm-referenced assessments can only provide information about the performance of one examinee relative to that of another.

Whether examinations and assessments should be designed to provide criterion-referenced or norm-referenced information about students' abilities and achievements, etc., depends ultimately upon the use to which the examination and assessment results are to be put. If the main purpose of the examination is to produce a ranking of examinees on the basis of their general performance, the use of norm-referenced tests is entirely appropriate. By contrast, if it is the function of an assessment to identify which particular skills are or are not possessed by an examinee, criterion-referenced testing procedures are called for.

Norm-referencing in Practice

Traditionally, most formal examinations – whether in the school sector (e.g. GCE and CSE examinations) or in Further and Higher Education – have tended to be norm-referenced, in that their main function is to separate students into distinct grade categories. In GCE A-level examinations, for example, candidates are distributed – on the basis of their overall performance – among five 'pass' grades, labelled respectively A, B, C, D and E, and two 'fail' categories, usually referred to as O and F. A typical distribution of candidates among these grades might be:

	Grade A	Top 10% of candidates
	Grade B	Next 15% of candidates
Pass grades	Grade C	Next 15% of candidates
	Grade D	Next 15% of candidates
	Grade E	Next 18% of candidates
Fail grades	O-Grade	Next 12% of candidates
	Grade F	Bottom 15% of candidates

Grade distribution profiles such as the foregoing vary in detail from subject to subject, but tend to be remarkably constant, for a given subject, from year to year. Table 3.4 illustrates this for the 1979 and 1980 A-level examinations, in Biology, Chemistry and Physics, of one of the major GCE Boards in England. The fact that approximately the same proportions of candidates are awarded particular grades, irrespective of the

Table 3.4. Grade distribution profiles for A-level examinations in different science subjects and in two different years

	Biology		Chemistry		Physics		All subjects	
Grade	1979	1980	1979	1980	1979	1980	1979	1980
A	10.1	10.2	11.8	10.5	10.0	10.7	9.8	10.0
B	15.5	13.9	14.7	16.6	18.3	15.9	16.0	15.9
C	12.9	13.1	12.5	11.5	12.4	13.6	13.8	14.2
D	14.1	14.6	15.9	16.4	13.3	12.8	15.7	16.1
E	18.2	17.9	18.9	17.1	19.7	21.0	17.5	17.4
A to E	70.8	69.7	73.8	72.1	73.7	74.0	72.8	73.6

Percentage of candidates receiving grades

subject taken, demonstrates clearly the norm-referenced nature of these examinations. Their essential purpose is to locate an individual candidate within the performance spectrum of all candidates examined, and to award to the candidate the grades that correspond to that location. For this to be carried out effectively, the test or examination should allow the maximum discrimination to be achieved between candidates of different performances.

In the technical sense, the term *discrimination* refers to the effectiveness of a test or examination to rank examinees as accurately as possible in the order of their attainments. The overall discrimination provided by a test depends on the discriminating power of the items of which it is composed. For an item to have a high discriminating power, it should be answered correctly by a high proportion of good students and incorrectly by a high proportion of poor students. Items for which this is not the case either do not contribute to the overall discriminatory power of the test or may – in exceptional circumstances – even have a negative effect upon it.

Generally, methods for the determination of item discrimination indices rely on the estimation of the correlation between students' performances on a particular test item and their performance on the test as a whole. Among the measures frequently used to express the discriminating power of an item are the biserial correlation coefficient and the point-biserial correlation coefficient. For detailed information on these and their calculation, reference should be made to appropriate textbooks on educational and psychological measurement. Suffice it here to indicate that discrimination indices can assume the range of values usually associated with correlation coefficients, viz. from +1 to −1.

In the design of actual tests or examinations intended for norm-referenced measurements, it is desirable for each item to have as high a discrimination index as possible. In practice, a lower limit of 0.30 is generally acceptable, although sometimes items of an even lower discrimination index may be incorporated in an examination, if this is justified for reasons of a high content validity (see Table 3.1).

A major factor affecting the discriminating power of a test item is its difficulty. For dichotomous test items, i.e. those that are marked as either correct or incorrect, the item difficulty index is usually defined as the proportion of correct answers obtained from the examined population. For non-dichotomous items that allow multiple marks to be awarded, the item difficulty is given by the ratio of the average score on the item to the maximum score possible.

In the strict sense, the terms item difficulty and difficulty index are misnomers in that they relate to what is essentially a measure of the ease of an item, or its *facility*. Consequently, the terms item facility and facility index are to be preferred.

To illustrate the influence of the facility of an item upon its discrimination, consider two dichotomous items having a facility of 1.00 and 0.00, respectively. The first of these is clearly so easy that it is answered correctly by *all* students, whilst the second proves too difficult for them. The result is that neither item is capable of discriminating between students of different attainment levels: each item has a discrimination index of zero.

Table 3.5 shows the approximate relationship between item facility and the maximum discrimination index that is obtainable on theoretical grounds. In practice, few items in a test or examination are found to have discrimination indices close to the theoretical values. The reason for this is often that an item fails to discriminate homogeneously across all ability or attainment levels determined by the test or examination.

It follows from the foregoing that, in the design of good norm-referenced examinations, close attention must be paid to the selection of items or tasks that discriminate effectively between students of different

Table 3.5. Relationship between item facility and maximum item discrimination

Item facility	0.0	0.1	0.2	0.3	0.4	0.5	0.6	0.7	0.8	0.9	1.0
Maximum discrimination index	0.0	0.2	0.4	0.6	0.8	1.0	0.8	0.6	0.4	0.2	0.0

ability. This, in turn, requires such items or tasks to have a facility level that makes them neither too easy nor too difficult for the examined population to answer. Whether this requirement is fulfilled depends not only on the test or examination itself but also on the characteristics of the examined population. For this reason, it has become customary for all major GCE and CSE Examination Boards to 'pretest' their examination questions and papers, using pretest populations of characteristics comparable to those of the population to be examined. In the main, though, such pretesting is confined to multiple-choice and short-answer examinations.

Some Issues Concerning Criterion-referencing

The major disadvantage of norm-referenced tests and examinations is that they merely rank candidates in order of attainment, without indicating the nature and level of the skills and abilities acquired by them. This limits the interpretability of examination and assessment results, and may even render them unhelpful in situations when detailed information about students' strengths and weaknesses is required. For example, in the assessment of a student's competence in operating a microscope, the relative performance of the student is of little interest. Instead, what matters is whether the student is capable of mounting a microscope slide, illuminating it to the best advantage, changing the objective to obtain an appropriate resolution and focusing the microscope.

The basic feature of criterion-referenced testing is that it seeks to establish whether a student can or cannot demonstrate particular kinds or levels of performance on items or tasks that describe the desired outcome of learning. An obvious prerequisite of this approach to testing is the clear identification of the tasks to be accomplished by the learner, including the specification of performance criteria. In general, this information may be derived from statements of educational objectives, provided that these give sound guidance to the attainments expected of students.

A particular problem concerns the ability to generalise the results derived from criterion-referenced examinations.The basic issue here is how one can ensure that each task incorporated in a criterion-related test is adequately representative of the task domain to which it relates. Assume, for example, that an assessment is to be made of a student's skills in carrying out simple physical measurements of, e.g. length, volume, mass, time, etc. To how many different test situations would the student have to be exposed before a reasonably reliable verdict could be given about his or her competence in this task domain?

From a theoretical point of view, this problem is solved if the criterion-referenced test incorporates the full range of tasks characteristic of a task domain. But such a solution proves usually impracticable: it is hardly possible for a single examination to probe into the total variety of learning outcomes expected of a course or a curriculum. Thus, some 'sampling' of tasks is necessary. However, as soon as this is the case, the ability to generalise the information derived from the examination is reduced. By comparison, this problem does not arise in norm-referenced examinations.

Much of the statistical information whereby the quality of norm-referenced tests or examinations can be judged cannot be applied to criterion-referenced measures. For example, the concepts of facility and discrimination are meaningless in the context of criterion-based tests. Likewise, the customary measures of reliability (cf. Table 3.2) are inapplicable to criterion-referenced tests, although some attempts have been made to develop formulae for the estimation of the reliability of these tests also.[2] Generally, the quality of criterion-referenced tests tends to be judged in terms of how closely the items and tasks correspond to those specified by, or implicit in, the objectives and criteria to which the assessment refers. However, it must also be stated that criterion-referencing has not so far found widespread application in educational testing and examining, although interest in it is rapidly gaining momentum. Some of the contemporary trends in this direction are discussed in Chapter 7.

Conclusion

Our concern in this chapter has been with a number of technical matters as they relate to examinations and assessment. First and foremost among these are the issues of validity and reliability, which together determine the quality of a test or examination paper. The question of what 'references' are available against which students' achievements or attainments can be measured has also been discussed and attention was drawn to an increasing interest in the adoption of criterion-referenced assessment procedures for school and public examinations.

Notes and References
1 E.F. Lindquist *A First Course in Statistics* Houghton Mifflin Co. (Boston, Mass.) 1942 (as quoted by R.L. Ebel *Measuring Educational Achievement* Prentice-Hall (Englewood Cliffs, NJ) 1965.
2 S.A. Livingstone 'Criterion-referenced applications of classical test theory.' *Journal of Educational Measurement*, Volume 9 (1972) pages 13–26.

The Assessment of Knowledge and Process Skills in Science

The development of students' cognitive skills and abilities has traditionally been regarded as the key function of the educational process. Science education is no exception in this respect, notwithstanding the fact that it is also concerned with the acquisition of practical, i.e. psychomotor skills. The relative importance attributed in science education to the two domains of ability and skill is readily seen from the relative weighting accorded to them in formal examinations: the weighting given to practical work rarely exceeds 20% and may be as low as 10%.[1]

The cognitive abilities that science education seeks to develop in students are fairly diverse in nature, and range from the acquisition and memorisation of factual knowledge to sophisticated problem-solving and evaluation skills. The first successful attempts to describe the full range of such skills and abilities were made in the early 1960s by the Nuffield O-level science curriculum development teams. They were largely based on the work of Bloom and coworkers, who had, in 1956, proposed a 'taxonomy of educational objectives for the cognitive domain'.[2] In this, they arranged educational objectives in hierarchical order so that a higher level objective automatically embraced a lower level objective.

Bloom's original taxonomy contains six different levels, but for most science examinations three of these tend to be combined, giving a four-level classification of the following type.

Level 1: *Knowledge and recall* of scientific facts, hypotheses, theories and concepts, as well as of terminology and convention.

Level 2: *Comprehension (understanding)* of scientific knowledge and relationships, which manifests itself in the student's ability to explain and interpret information presented and to express it in alternative communication modes.

Level 3: *Application* of scientific knowledge and understanding to unfamiliar, i.e. novel, situations. The ability to apply knowledge implies that the student is able to select from his knowledge reservoir those items of knowledge and relationships that are relevant to the novel situation.

Level 4:[3] *Analysis, synthesis and evaluation* of scientific information, which involves the breaking down of information into its constituent parts (analysis) and reorganising it so that a new structure emerges (synthesis). Additionally, the information may have to be evaluated in terms of its validity or underlying assumptions, and consequences.

As was already indicated in Chapter 2, ability categories like the foregoing are now widely used, together with appropriate subject content categories, to form 'grids' which specify the requirements of an examination. Figure 2.1 (page 28) is an example of one such grid.

As to techniques available for the assessment of the various skills and abilities embraced by the above categories, these have already been reviewed in Chapter 2 and their main strengths and weaknesses described. Hence, no further discussion of these techniques is necessary. Instead, we shall focus, in this chapter, on three issues that have a direct bearing on the design of examinations whereby students' knowledge and process skills in science can be measured. These are:

– the assessment of science process skills;
– the assessment of communication skills, and
– the effect, on student performance, of language and information level used in questions.

In all these, the focus will be on written examinations and assessments, since these represent by far the most important types.

Assessing Process Skills in Science

As was pointed out in Chapter 1, considerable emphasis is being given in contemporary science education to the acquisition, by the learner, of science process skills and abilities. Table 1.3 (page 13) presents a fairly comprehensive list of such skills.

Science process skills generally divide between those that are cognitive in nature (i.e. concern intellectual abilities) and those that relate to practical activities. Manipulative and observational skills, for example, belong to the latter category, whilst the recall and application of knowledge, the interpretation of information and problem-solving are examples of cognitive skills. It should be noted that the distinction between cognitive and practical (psychomotor) skills is frequently only a matter of convenience, for in many actual situations encountered in science education they come together. For example, to be able to 'follow instructions accurately for the conduct of experiments' (Table 1.3) may be a skill that relates primarily to the execution of a practical task, but also involves a significant cognitive element.

Our concern in this section is exclusively with the assessment of those science process skills that fall into the 'cognitive domain'. In general,

Table 4.1. Main science process skill items for assessment in the 'cognitive' domain

Category	Subcategory
I. Translation of information from one form into another	– reading information from graphs, tables and charts; – representing information in the form of graphs, tables and charts.
II. Explanation, interpretation and application of information	– explaining familiar facts, observations and phenomena in terms of scientific laws, theories and models; – recognition of patterns and relationships from experimental or other data; – suggesting scientific explanations of unfamiliar facts, observations and phenomena; – applying scientific ideas and procedures to solve qualitative and quantitative problems.
III. Planning of investigations	– recognising or proposing problems for investigation; – identifying variables to be examined and variables which need to be controlled; – devising or selecting experimental procedures appropriate to the investigation to be performed; – recognising potential sources of variability and error in experimental measurements.

these may be divided into the categories and subcategories shown in Table 4.1. The main categories correspond closely to those adopted by the APU Science Monitoring exercise;[4] the subcategory descriptions are, however, somewhat different from those used by the APU.

Skills and abilities appearing within the first two categories of the process skills can readily be located within the taxonomic levels based on Bloom's analysis (see above). In consequence, they may be adequately assessed by means of a range of techniques now well established in science education, e.g. multiple-choice item, and short-answer and structured questions. For relatively complex tasks, free-response questions offer considerable scope for interpretational and application (including problem-solving) abilities to be assessed, but attention is drawn to the observations made in Chapter 2.

In connection with their attempts to assess pupils' interpretation and application abilities (of the type given in Category II in Table 4.1), the APU Science Monitoring teams have developed a series of ingenious questions and test items. Their particular feature is that many of these explore 'everyday' situations and do not therefore require the pupil to possess specialised scientific knowledge. The following two examples are typical of this range of questions.

Example 1

The map shows the distribution of mushrooms in a meadow.

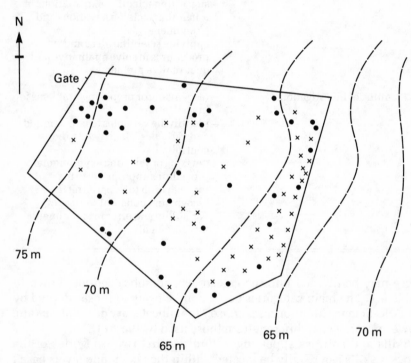

KEY:

⌒ = Contour lines to show the height of the land

• = Position of 5–day old cow droppings

× = Position of mushrooms

It is claimed that *mushrooms prefer to grow in damp soil.*
Study the map carefully. Explain how the map either supports or does not support this claim:

....

....

....

....

Example 2

Mr Brown had a garden full of daffodils, crocuses and snowdrops, which came up year after year.

Daffodil	Crocus	Snowdrop

For three years Mr Brown kept a record of when the plants were in flower. This is what it looked like.

	EARLY JAN.	LATE JAN.	EARLY FEB.	LATE FEB.	EARLY MARCH	LATE MARCH	EARLY APRIL	LATE APRIL	EARLY MAY
YEAR 1		snowdrop	crocus+snowdrop	crocus	daffodil+crocus	daffodil	daffodil	daffodil	
YEAR 2					snowdrop	crocus+snowdrop	crocus	daffodil+crocus	daffodil
YEAR 3				crocus	crocus	daffodil+crocus	daffodil	daffodil	daffodil

(Mr Brown forgot to put snowdrops on the record in year 3!)

(a) What pattern do you notice in the chart about the times at which crocuses and daffodils flowered?

....

....

....

(b) When do you think the snowdrops were in flower during year 3?

....

For the assessment, by means of written tests, of students' abilities to design experiments and plan investigations (cf. Category III, Table 4.1), two basic approaches offer themselves:

i The student is presented with information about an experimental design and asked to evaluate or criticise it. This may include situations where the student may have to choose one of a number of possible lines of action and justify the choice made.
ii The student is given a problem to be investigated and then required to propose an appropriate experimental procedure. This may include the identification of variables that have to be controlled, a recommendation about the quantities to be measured and the evaluation of the results, etc.

These approaches can in principle be applied both to entire investigations or to parts thereof, as has been successfully demonstrated by the APU. Examples 3 and 4 illustrate the two approaches. They are concerned with the assessment of students' ability to identify variables that have to be controlled in an experiment.

In Example 3, a multiple-choice format is used, which corresponds to situation (i) above. In Example 4, which corresponds to situation (ii), the student has to generate a suitable set of answers. In either case, however, the tasks to be accomplished by the student are well-defined and lead to answers that can be assessed with a high degree of objectivity and reliability.

Example 3

Some materials are said to be better conductors of electricity than others.

Mandy is given a circuit like the one in the diagram so that she can find out whether this statement is correct. She can measure how well each material conducts by comparing the brightness of the bulb.

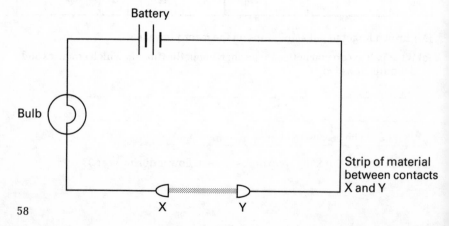

Which of the following should she do?
Put a *tick* in the box by the things she must keep the *same*.
Put a *cross* in the box by the things she must *change*.

☐ A   The number of batteries used in the circuit.

☐ B   The kind of bulb in the holder.

☐ C   The kind of material used for the strip.

☐ D   The thickness of the material used for the strip.

☐ E   The number of bulbs used in the circuit.

Example 4

Kelly noticed that when celery stalks were put in coloured ink, the ink travelled up the stems and could be seen in the veins of the leaves.

She wanted to find out if *the thickness of the celery stalks made a difference to how quickly the ink travelled up the stem*.

(a) To find this out, what things should she be sure to keep the *same*?

....

....

(b) What must she be sure to *change* in order to find out the answer?

....

....

As far as these approaches are concerned, it should be noted that, although they appear equivalent to each other in terms of *face validity*, they are not necessarily equivalent in terms of the student performances to which they give rise. This is an issue yet to be explored through appropriate investigations.

The assessment of the planning of entire investigations is usually less straightforward than that of simple component tasks of the planning process, for the following reasons:

i The student may have to make assumptions about the range of facilities and apparatus that would be available to him, and about the desired accuracy of the results.

ii Likewise, the student may have to make *a priori* judgements about what aspects of the investigation should be explicitly referred to in the plan and what can be taken for granted.

As a result of these two factors, students may perceive a given planning task in somewhat different ways, with the consequence that they concentrate on different aspects. The task thus assumes an 'open-ended' character.

It is of course possible to eliminate or, at least, reduce the open-endedness of elaborate planning tasks by specifying, as part of the task description, the boundary conditions to be attached to it and also the particular planning issues that the student is to consider. Example 5, which is based on one of the APU planning tasks, shows how this can be done. In the original formulation of the question, the items of equipment were shown in the form of pictorial representations. The initial part of this example would represent the planning task in an open-ended format.

Example 5

You are provided with three different kinds of paper towel, X, Y and Z. Describe an experiment that you could do in order to find out:
'Which kind of paper can hold the most water?'

In your answer you should write about:
  – the things you would use,
  – the quantities you would measure and how you would measure them,
  – what you would do to make it a 'fair' test,
  – how you would work out your results.

You may assume that you will have access to the following equipment:
Beakers,
Measuring cylinders, small and large size,
Ruler and scissors,
Filter funnels,
Petri dishes,
Water tray and water,
Scales for weighing,

Rolls of the paper towels, X, Y and Z,
Stopwatch.

Even if problems are so designed that they inform students about, for example, boundary conditions and aspects of the planning task to be considered, they still offer much scope for different approaches to be proposed. For example, in relation to the foregoing problem, the approaches advocated by students participating in the APU Science Monitoring included the following:

(a) Find/compare amount of water soaked up by towel from a larger quantity of water.
(b) Find/compare amount of water squeezed or dripped out from fully soaked paper.
(c) Find/compare amount of water soaked up by paper previously soaked and squeezed.
(d) Find/compare amount of water needed to soak the paper.
(e) Find/compare how much paper was needed to soak up water.
(f) Find the time taken for paper to become soaked.
(g) Find the time taken for the water to be soaked up.

The evaluation of answers falling within these categories can pose further problems. Some of the students' proposals may readily be regarded as 'unreasonable' or 'impractical' and, hence, be deemed to be unsatisfactory. Others, however, may be entirely sound in principle, in that they would allow the problem to be solved; yet, even these may differ in 'quality': the likelihood of one approach giving reproducible quantitative results may be greater than that of another. Consequently, if assessments are to be made for grading purposes, teachers and examiners may have to set up their own merit ratings for different kinds of answers.

In listing the 'planning of investigations' among the qualities that can be assessed by means of written questions (or other techniques appropriate to the assessment of cognitive abilities), a very important assumption has been made. This is that students' performances on 'planning' questions appearing in a written format reflect fairly accurately the planning skills that they would display in actual practical problem-solving situations, e.g. in the laboratory or in the 'field'. Recent APU findings suggest that this assumption may not be fully justified.[5] In connection with its monitoring at age 13, the APU examined pupils' performances on a limited number of identical planning tasks in the context of (i) written tests and (ii) laboratory investigations.

The relevant APU report does not make any comparison (e.g. by means of correlational data) between pupil performances under the two conditions, but points to several general differences between answers obtained in the two contexts. These may be summarised thus:

- Pupils' ability to express themselves adequately in writing can have a significant effect upon the quality of answers obtained via the written assessment mode.
- When producing written answers, pupils have to decide what details of the actions planned have to be explicitly listed in their report and which can be assumed to be unnecessary (because they would be understood by the assessor to be implicit).

It must be left to further investigations to establish how significant the differences in performance are when planning tasks are attended to in different settings. That such differences occur is, however, beyond doubt and this points strongly to the importance of pupils' communication and language skills as determinants of their performance.

Assessing Communication Skills

The development of students' ability to communicate scientific ideas in a clear and logical form and to write on matters of scientific interest has long been an accepted goal of science education at all levels. The recently published 16+ National Criteria for Science endorse this particular point:[6]

Students are expected to demonstrate the skill and ability . . . to communicate scientific observations, ideas and arguments logically, concisely and in various forms.

Despite the wide-ranging and long-standing agreement about the importance of communication skills within the total framework of science process skills, few genuine attempts have been made so far to evolve procedures and criteria for their assessment. It is true that a few GCE Boards have attempted to allow for the assessment of communication skills within the framework of their O-level science examinations, as is evidenced by the London Board, which currently states in the rubric for the essay-question section in its O-level Chemistry examination (University of London 1983):[7]

One objective of this section is to give you the opportunity to organise material and present ideas, including calculations and diagrams where appropriate, in a clear and logical form. Approximately one third of the marks in Section B will be awarded for these aspects of your answers.

However, apart from this statement, no further information is provided by the London Board about the marking itself nor about the criteria which are considered in this.

Without doubt, free-response (essay-type) questions form the obvious context in which students' communication skills manifest themselves. This is indeed one of the major arguments in favour of their retention in formal examinations. Nevertheless, it would be futile to attempt to assess such skills unless a suitable set of criteria can be evolved whereby they can be judged.

A useful attempt in this direction was made by L'Odiaga, who considered five main qualities in the marking of answers to essay-type examination questions.[8] These were:

i The *correctness* of the scientific information presented by the student in the answer given.
ii The *relevance* of this information to the issue or problem under consideration.
iii The *logicality* of the argument presented and/or the conclusions reached.
iv The *organisation* or *sequencing* of the answer in relation to the component tasks associated with the question.
v The *clarity of expression* in the students' communication.

In assessing these qualities in a representative sample of A-level Chemistry questions, L'Odiaga used impressionistic marking on a five-point rating scale. This approach was in line with that advocated by Mathews,[9] and not only proved useful but also produced an acceptable level of concordance between different markers. Thus, it can certainly be recommended for use by teachers and examiners who seek to assess students' communication skills.

Effect of Language and Information Level on Test Performance

Language is of central importance in all aspects of examinations and assessments. It is the means through which teachers and examiners transmit examination tasks to students; likewise, it forms the principal mode whereby students communicate their answers. Thus, the question arises to what extent, if any, students' performances on examination tasks are affected by the way in which the tasks are formulated.

In an investigation reported in 1977, Cassels and Johnstone administered two sets of multiple-choice questions to nearly 2000 O-grade Chemistry students in Scotland. One set consisted of questions similar to those used in the Scottish Certificate of Education Examination; the other set presented the same questions in a simplified format that had been achieved by the substitution of 'difficult' words by less difficult ones, or the removal of words or by sentence reorganisation.[10]

The effect of even relatively simple alterations on question facility was remarkable, as the examples in Table 4.2 illustrate. In the first three examples, the modifications concerned only the item stems, not the responses. The latter are therefore not shown, for brevity's sake. It may clearly be seen that, in every case, the simplified version of an item has a high facility value, which means that a larger percentage of the popula-

Table 4.2. Effect of language simplifications on the facility of test items

Type of alteration	Original version of item or item stem	Item facility	Simplified version of item or item stem	Item facility
Replacement of 'difficult' words by less difficult ones	Which of the following is *not* a pungent gas?	0.80	Which one of the following is *not* a choking gas?	0.95
	Which gas has diatomic molecules?	0.42	Which gas has two atoms in every molecule?	0.62
Removal of words	The atomic weights of most of the naturally occurring elements are not whole numbers. Which of the following is the best explanation of this fact?	0.48	Why are the atomic weights of naturally occurring elements not whole numbers?	0.53
Removal of words, plus sentence reconstruction	Which statement is true about the ions $^8_3Li^+$ and $^8_4Be^{2+}$? A. They contain the same number of neutrons. B. Their atoms contain the same number of protons. C. They will combine with the same number of + ions. D. They contain the same number of electrons.	0.31	$^8_3Li^+$ and $^8_4Be^{2+}$ have the same number of: A. neutrons B. protons C. charges D. electrons	0.43

Source: J.R.T. Cassels and A.H. Johnstone 'Language in chemistry' in *Research for the Classroom and Beyond – Report of a Symposium* The Chemical Society [now Royal Society of Chemistry] (London) 1977 pages 48–54.

tion was able to answer it correctly, compared with the item in its original form.

In their publication, Cassels and Johnstone point to other kinds of modification by which item facilities can be improved but recognise that this is a field for further research: 'It would be useful to be able to predict how certain linguistic constructions (in test items) would influence performance and this would assist in the preparation of multiple-choice questions.'

Following broadly similar lines to those of Cassels and Johnstone, Slimming (1984) has recently investigated the effect of information level in structured questions on students' performances.[11] The starting point to this was the claim, frequently made, that increasing the information presented in an examination task (by, for example, establishing a 'context' for the task) provides the students with potential clues to the answer and may, hence, enhance their chances of success. This argument can be supported, on theoretical grounds, by consideration of the relationship between students' problem-solving skills and their knowledge structure.

Starting from 'standard' examination-type structured questions, Slimming produced a number of questions that, compared with the standard items, were either significantly 'reduced' in content, or 'augmented' by additional information. Such additional information was of two types: it could be irrelevant to the task under consideration, so merely forming some 'embellishment' to the task itself; or it could be relevant to the problem-solving task and, hence, might provide the student with help in solving it.

Figure 4.1 shows the relationship between these levels of information. It may be seen that, as the information content of the test items increases, we proceed from the 'reduced item' type to the 'augmented item' category, with its subdivisions.

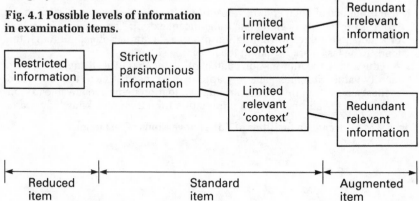

Fig. 4.1 Possible levels of information in examination items.

The essential characteristic of a 'reduced item' is that, unlike any other kind of item, it fails to present essential information required for the problem-solving task. Such information must thus be provided by the student himself, through appropriate assumptions being made. For example, even in the simplest case of a 'recall-type' task requiring the name of a process to be given, a 'reduced' version is possible when the process itself is inadequately characterised in the item. Table 4.3 presents a simple example of an examination item in different forms.

Table 4.3. Example of a simple test item presented at different levels of information content (schematic)

General item stem
Give the name of the industrial processes which involve the following:

(Standard version)	i	The catalytic reduction of nitrogen to ammonia
(Augmented, Relevant)	ii	The catalytic reduction of nitrogen to ammonia, using a catalyst of finely divided iron with promoters
(Augmented, Irrelevant)	iii	The catalytic reduction of nitrogen to ammonia, in the gaseous phase
(Reduced version)	iv	The catalytic reduction of nitrogen

Source: D. Slimming 'Problem-solving in the context of the GCE Ordinary Level Advanced Chemistry examination.' Ph.D. thesis (University of Keele) 1984.

The effect of information level on student performance was evaluated by means of facility values calculated for the various test items in their different versions. Figure 4.2 shows the results for some 15 item-pairs for which the statistical significance of the difference between facility values was at least 5%. For other item-pairs, the general trends were similar, though without necessarily reaching the 5% significance level.

The findings resulting from this study may be summarised thus:

i The influence of *augmented irrelevant* information is frequently such that it reduces the facility of an item to a significant extent. The presence in an item of augmented relevant information produces a similar effect, although this tends to be less marked than in the foregoing situation.

ii A reduction in the information content of an item has little, if any, effect on its facility value. Students generally appear to be insensitive to the removal of modest amounts of information from examination items and are able to compensate for the absence of such information from their own knowledge base.

Fig. 4.2 Main trends in facilities of different versions of test items.

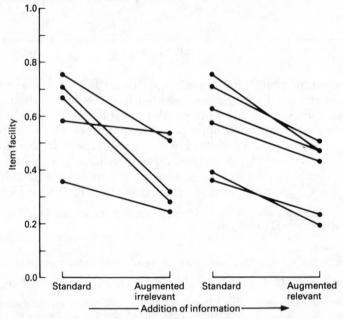

Closer analysis of students' answers enabled Slimming to draw a further conclusion in relation to the findings under (i). This was that the effect of augmentation of information was not uniform for all achievement groups, but that it affected mainly the average and below average performers. These students showed a strong tendency to employ each and every piece of information presented in an item, in their personal attempts to solve it. In this way, any additional information, even when this should have been helpful, proved distracting and confusing.

In the light of this finding, the original notion, that information enhancement should help students, cannot be upheld.

Conclusion

The intention in this chapter was to deal in detail with a limited number of issues in the assessment of cognitive abilities in science, rather than to provide a comprehensive survey of all relevant assessment techniques.

The issues chosen for special consideration were the assessment of science process skills and of communication skills, as well as the influence of language and information level used in examination questions on student performance.

As the discussion will have indicated, in all these areas important questions still arise and call for further research and development work. The issue of language and information content used in examination questions merits particular attention and should be foremost in the minds of teachers and examiners.

Notes and References
1 For the new GCSE examinations to be introduced in 1988, a minimum weighting of 20% has been specified for experimental and other practical skills. At least half of these marks must be awarded for experimental and observable work in the laboratory or its equivalent.
2 B.S. Bloom (editor) *Taxonomy of Educational Objectives: Handbook 1, Cognitive Domain* Longmans (London and New York) 1956.
3 Bloom and coworkers place 'analysis', 'synthesis' and 'evaluation' at three separate levels. In many practical applications of the taxonomy, e.g. in examination design, they are combined into a single level of 'higher intellectual abilities'.
4 Department of Education and Science (DES) *The Assessment Framework for Science at Ages 13 and 15. APU Science Report for Teachers* No. 2 Department of Education and Science (London) 1984.
5 DES *Science in Schools. Age 13: Report* No. 2 Department of Education and Science (London) 1984.
6 DES *GCSE (General Certificate of Secondary Education) – The National Criteria* HMSO (London) 1985.
7 Copies of past examination papers are obtainable from the University of London Publications Office, Gordon Square, London WC1.
8 J. L'Odiaga 'A feasibility study of criterion-referenced grading in the context of GCE Advanced Level Chemistry examinations.' M.Sc. thesis (University of Keele) 1977.
9 Nuffield Advanced Science *Examinations and Assessment* Penguin (Harmondsworth, Middlesex) 1972.
10 J.R.T. Cassels and A.H. Johnstone 'Language in chemistry' in *Research for the Classroom and Beyond – Report of a Symposium* The Chemical Society [now Royal Society of Chemistry] (London) 1977 pages 48–54.
11 D. Slimming 'Problem-solving in the context of the GCE Ordinary Level Advanced Chemistry examination.' Ph.D. thesis (University of Keele) 1984.

5

The Assessment of Practical Abilities

It is widely recognised and acknowledged that all sciences have an empirical basis and that they involve practical pursuits and activities. In some of the sciences, especially the usual physical sciences, practical activities tend to be laboratory-based and experimental in nature; in other sciences, for example the earth sciences, including astronomy, practical activities often tend to be fieldwork-based and depend less on actual experimentation, but none the less involve careful observation and deduction. (Here, experimentation means an investigative process that involves the setting up of an experiment and the deliberate control of variables.)

The view has long been established, particularly in British science education, that the development of practical skills and abilities must form an integral part of the set of educational goals that is to be associated with science education. Thus, practical work has traditionally played a key part in all our science education programmes, including those designed for the school level. This has manifested itself in the fairly extensive provision, in all our educational institutions, of laboratories and other facilities required for practical work in the sciences. It should be noted in passing that other countries, e.g. the USA, France and Germany, have developed traditions of science education at school level in which rather less emphasis is placed on practical work than is the case in Britain.[1]

A number of different reasons and justifications can be cited in support of a laboratory- or fieldwork-based approach to science education. Some of these reflect the view taken of the nature of science (e.g. 'science is a practical subject and depends for its progress on practical work and experimentation'); others bring educational reasons into the foreground (e.g. 'practical work has a motivating effect upon students' or 'exposure to practical experiences enhances students' understanding of scientific phenomena and concepts'). These and other, related reasons represent the scenario within which practical work is undertaken in science education. However, they do not normally express the particular achievements and outcomes that are expected of practical work at school level. These are in the main concerned with the range of skills and competences that are regarded as essential components of practical work in science.

The Nature of Practical Skills and Abilities

We may define practical skills and abilities as those that form an integral part of any investigative process in science and through which the investigator obtains first-hand experience of some scientific phenomenon or relationship. In general, the following broad stages are associated with experimental work in science:

i The perception and formulation of a problem to be solved by practical means.
ii The design and planning of an experimental procedure for solving the problem.
iii The setting up of the experiment and its execution.
iv The conduct of measurements and/or observations and their systematic recording.
v The interpretation and evaluation of the experimental observations and data.

Depending on the nature of the particular problem under investigation (which, in turn, tends often to be determined by the direction of enquiry characteristic of a particular science discipline), these foregoing stages can vary from case to case. This is especially true for the 'experimentation' stage (stage iii), as pointed out above. There may also be variations in the importance that is attached to these various components of practical work in the educational context. For example, problem recognition and formulation – though intrinsically important – are often omitted from a list of components of experimental work, since they are held to be skills in which little, if any, mastery can be expected of pupils and school students. Thus, for example, the schemes for the assessment of practical skills in the various sciences at the GCE A-level, issued by the GCE Boards, make no reference to the first of the phases, although the remaining four feature in several schemes.[2]

Of the five activity areas represented by the above stages, only (iii) and (iv) are genuinely 'practical' in nature, in that they involve the actual handling of materials and equipment. The other activities, viz. (i), (ii) and (v), have strong 'theoretical' orientation: although they form an integral part of experimental work, they do not involve or depend upon the exercise of manipulative and observations skills. For this reason, it is widely accepted that abilities and skills associated with these activities can readily be assessed by means of written tests and examinations. Most examination boards regularly incorporate into their theory examination questions designed to test students' knowledge about experimental procedures and their ability to interpret data and information. The APU, likewise, has adopted this approach, e.g. for the purpose of testing pupils' skills in designing and planning investigations. This aspect was discussed in Chapter 4.

If the components of experimental work in science are to be satisfactorily assessed, it is necessary to evolve at least some broad qualities with reference to which students' performances can be judged. Table 5.1 presents a summary of such qualities. These can, of course, serve only as a general framework for development of more specific assessment criteria.

Table 5.1. Qualities for consideration in the development of schemes for the assessment of practical abilities

Ability/skill to be assessed	General qualities for assessment
(a) Recognition and formulation of problem	Tenability of hypotheses and postulates; identification of variables to be studied; identification of variables to be controlled.
(b) Design and planning of experimental procedure	Choice of experimental conditions, including choice of apparatus and measuring techniques and procedures; arrangements for varying and controlling variables; sequencing of operations, etc.
(c) Setting-up and execution of experimental work (manipulation)	Methodical working; correctness and safety of experimental technique, manual dexterity in the execution of practical work; orderliness and organisation.
(d) Observational and measuring skills (including the recording of data and observations)	Accuracy and precision in the conduct of measurements; reliability of observations. Care and reliability in the collection and recording of data and observations.
(e) Interpretation and evaluation of experimental data and observations	Tenability of conclusions and inferences drawn from experimental data, and their relevance to the problem under investigation. Evaluation of limitations and potential error sources associated with experimental procedure.

Table 5.2. A breakdown analysis of manipulative skills

Skill competence	Performance features
Methodical working	Correct sequencing of tasks forming part of an overall operation. Effective and purposeful utilisation of equipment. Efficient use of working time. Ability to develop an acceptable working procedure on the basis of limited instruction.
Experimental techniques	Correct handling of apparatus and materials. Safe execution of an experimental procedure. Taking of adequate precautions to ensure reliable observations and results.
Manual dexterity	Swift and confident manner of execution of practical task. Successful completion of an operation or its constituent part-tasks.
Orderliness	Good utilisation of available working (laboratory bench) space. Organisation in the placing of equipment and materials used. Tidiness of the working area.

To illustrate how the scheme put forward in Table 5.1 can be elaborated to yield more precise points for use in the assessment of practical skills, we may consider the area of 'manipulative' skills (ability/skills area). In an attempt to develop operational assessment criteria for this area, Eglen and Kempa proposed the breakdown analysis shown in Table 5.2.[3] This led to a number of general performance features in relation to the exercise of manipulative skills that, as the authors were able to demonstrate, could readily be applied to particular practical tasks selected for assessment purposes. Similar breakdown analyses, yielding generalised assessment criteria, can be developed for the other ability/skills areas listed in Table 5.1.

The five phases of experimental work summarized in Table 5.1 are now widely recognised as forming a valid and satisfactory framework within which practical skills are to be developed and assessed. It is clear from this that practical skills cannot be thought of simply as representing 'psychomotor' skills, i.e. those involving manipulation and observation. Instead, they cover all activities that form part of a genuine investigative

Fig. 5.1 Schematic problem-solving model for practical investigations.
Source: **Based on the model proposed by the APU Science Monitoring team (cf. DES *The Assessment Framework for Science at Ages 13 and 15. APU Science Report for Teachers No. 2* Department of Education and Science (London) 1984.**

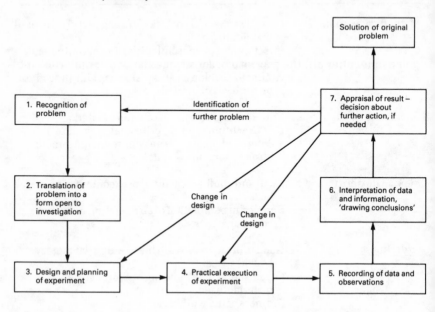

process, from the conception of a problem to its solution by practical means. This emphasis on problem-solving is very aptly brought out in a model of a problem-solving chain that has been used by the APU[4] as the basis of its assessment of pupils' performance of practical investigations. The APU model is shown in Fig. 5.1, in a modified form.

The interesting feature of the APU model is that it views the investigative process as a dynamic one, in the course of which the experimenter may adjust or modify his strategy and method of investigation. This is clearly expressed by the incorporation in the model of a number of 'feedback' loops, including one that allows for the possible reappraisal of the problem itself.

Should Outcomes or Processes be Assessed?

By and large, the qualities suggested in Table 5.1 for the development of schemes of assessment of practical abilities refer to the processes involved in the conduct of investigations. They are therefore *process skills* that we may associate with practical work. Any assessment procedure based on some or all of these qualities must inevitably be biased towards the *process* dimension of practical work. The question to be raised now is whether this kind of bias can be justified or whether the assessment of practical work should be oriented towards the other, non-process criteria.

The obvious alternative to the use of process-related assessment criteria is to focus on the *outcomes* of practical work. This is entirely defensible: after all, the purpose of most practical work undertaken by pupils and students is to give rise to observations and data that can be meaningfully interpreted and evaluated. Thus, the success of a practical activity manifests itself in the quality of the results obtained from it. In other words, might one not argue that the quality of a student's practical work is only as good as the quality of his or her results? It should be noted that, traditionally, the assessment of students' practical abilities in science subjects has been based on the outcomes of practical exercises carried out by them, the assumption being that a high correlation exists between the results achieved by them and the quality of their practical processes.

A number of studies undertaken in recent years suggests that this correlation is far from high. For example, Buckley compared practical grades awarded on the basis of the results of laboratory exercises in A-level Chemistry with those based upon the direct observation of students' practical performances on the same exercises.[5] The average correlation found by him between the two sets of grades was 0.25, and in no single case did the correlation coefficient exceed 0.35. Similarly, low correlations were found to exist between grades for practical abilities derived from 'internal' teacher-based assessments and from formal 'external' practical examinations, respectively.[6] The conclusion to be drawn from findings such as these is that we cannot simply infer a student's practical competence from the outcomes of practical exercises. Likewise, 'good results' obtained in practical work are in themselves not necessarily indicative of good practical skills.

The lack of a close relationship between the quality of the outcomes achieved in practical work and the quality of the procedure used in it is not difficult to explain. Most practical exercises and tasks in science readily divide into a number of subtasks, each of which can be subject to procedural errors and inaccuracies. It is not impossible for a relatively minor error in one of the subtasks to affect adversely the final outcome of the overall exercise, even if all other subtasks have been carried out satisfactorily. Similarly, it is not impossible that errors committed in several subtasks compensate one another, with the effect that an 'acceptable' result is obtained without the practical performance itself having been satisfactory.

To illustrate this point, consider a simple volumetric chemical exercise involving the following subtasks:

Weighing of a solid for making a standard solution.
Preparation of the standard solution.
Washing and filling of burette.
Pipetting and transfer of solution(s) other than the standard solution.
Titration procedure.

Assume that, in the course of the weighing operation, a student fails to read the balance scale correctly or that he records the weight wrongly. If the error remains undetected by the student, the final result of the titration exercise will be inaccurate: even complete perfection in the execution of all other subtasks will not correct this. Now suppose that another student, carrying out the same exercise, (i) spills some of the weighed solid during the preparation of the standard solution, and (ii) overshoots the titration end-point. Both errors, though very significant in themselves, tend to compensate each other and this can lead to an 'acceptable' result being returned on the basis of a less than satisfactory working procedure.

The observed discrepancy between outcome-based and process-based assessments of practical work in science leads to the important question of which criterion should be adopted in determining students' practical skills and abilities. The answer to this must ultimately depend on value judgements. If the viewpoint expressed by Chalmers and Stark is accepted that 'the only significant criterion of good experimental work lies in the result it achieves',[7] any assessment of practical skills should be based on outcome-related criteria. However, if one accepts or prefers the counter-argument, that it is more important that students should develop sound investigative abilities, including manipulative skills and working habits, the decision would have to be in favour of a (predominantly) process-based assessment of practical work.

Contemporary practice is far from uniform in this respect. A number of GCE Boards, for example, offer schools the choice of entering their A-level science students for 'externally' conducted practical examinations, or conducting 'internal' teacher-based assessments of practical abilities. Given the conditions under which external examinations are normally conducted (three-hour time restriction and standardised experiments), grades and marks arrived at from this assessment mode are inevitably 'outcome-related'. Since assessments made by this mode rely generally on the evaluation of written information (notes, observations, data and measurements, as well as diagrams) prepared by the student in the course of the examination, they cannot adequately encompass the 'process' aspects of practical work referred to above.

By comparison, teacher-based procedures for the assessment of practical work generally allow students' process skills, e.g. in the manipulative sphere, to be measured in a satisfactory manner – usually through the adoption of assessment procedures involving the direct observation of students' performances. This should increase the validity of such assessments over those which are 'outcome-based'. This must be seen as a definite advantage of the teacher-based assessment mode over the traditional practical examination, although the implementation of the former can give rise to certain organisational problems. In most cases, though, teachers have successfully overcome them.

To summarise: a crucial issue in the assessment of students' practical skills and abilities is whether such assessment should be based on the outcomes of practical work or on the evaluation of the processes skills that are involved in the practical task. Which basis is accepted and adopted for the assessment is likely to depend on the perceived purpose of the practical work, but may also be a matter of personal value judgement. Indeed, in certain situations it may be possible to combine process-based and outcome-based assessments. However, it should be noted that, normally, assessments and grades arrived at by the two modes are not comparable and are only weakly correlated.

Developing Criteria for the Assessment of Practical Skills

Irrespective of whether the evaluation of students' practical abilities and skills is based on an assessment of outcomes or processes, it is important that the assessor employs sound and operationally meaningful assessment criteria. The purpose of this section is to discuss and illustrate how such criteria may be developed. It is expedient in this context to deal separately with outcome-based and with process-related assessment criteria.

Outcome-based Assessment Criteria

In considering the outcomes or results obtained from practical work, we may broadly distinguish between those which express some *quantitative* value or relationship and those that are *qualitative* in nature. In either case, the development of assessment criteria is relatively easy, at least in principle. For quantitative data, derived from a measurement or an estimation of some quantity, it is customary first to establish some 'target' value that is accepted as 'correct'. This value is then used as a reference against which the students' actual results are judged. Marks or grades are then awarded on the basis of how close a student's result is to the target value. The following two examples illustrate this.

Example 1. Assessment of volumetric exercises, e.g. in A-level Chemistry

Volumetric (titrimetric) exercises of the type included in practical examinations in chemistry are generally assessed on the basis of mark scales like the following:

Deviation of titration result from 'reference' or 'target' titre (cm^3)	Percentage of available marks awarded
< 0.10	100
< 0.15	80
< 0.20	60
< 0.25	40
< 0.30	20
≥ 0.30	0

The deviation bands can, of course, be adjusted if the nature of an exercise warrants this.

Example 2. Estimation of physical quantities

Several of the APU science studies have included questions requiring pupils to estimate the magnitude of certain physical quantities, such as length, area, volume, temperature, mass and force. The type of task given to pupils is illustrated by the following example, adapted from the second Age 15 Report of the APU:[8]

'You are to make your best guess at the answers to these questions.
You are not allowed to use measuring instruments.

a. What is the length of the rod labelled A? ..... cm
b. What is the volume of the bottle labelled B? ..... cm^3
c. What is the area of the bottom of bottle B? ..... cm^2
d. (In the case of a light switched on for a limited time interval)
   How long is the light on for? ..... sec
e. Pull the given elastic band to point E (marked on a scale).
   How much force is needed? ..... N.'

The scoring procedure adopted by the APU team was to award 'two marks for each estimate within a narrow range of the target value and one for an estimate within a wider range', although the range widths were not stated in the report.

The assessment of qualitative information obtained from practical work in science usually involves dichotomous judgements. In the marking of observational exercises, for example, the key issue is to establish whether the student has actually noticed a particular characteristic or feature of the system or change under scrutiny. Depending on whether a correct observation is reported or not, the mark is either awarded or withheld.

Assessment schemes developed on this basis have been successfully employed for a wide range of different tasks. For example, in a study of the performance of O-level Chemistry students on observational tasks of varying complexity undertaken by Ward,[9] the students were required to note and record any changes (in colour, temperature, state, etc.) associated with a series of different chemical reactions. The number of changes occurring more or less simultaneously in a reaction could vary from two to seven. In the marking of exercises, one mark was awarded for each correctly reported observation.

The students themselves were not aware of the total number of observations that was possible on each particular exercise; therefore, no upper limit as such was imposed upon them as to the number of observations to be reported. This led to the interesting situation that observational errors made by the students were not simply 'errors of omission' (where a student had failed to notice a particular change), but also 'illusory errors' (where an observation was claimed to have been made which, in practice, could not have been possible).

A further example of the use of a dichotomous scoring procedure is the following, which is reported in the APU Science study at Age 13.[10] In a specially designed observational exercise, pupils were provided with five tadpoles at different stages of development (sealed in separate specimen tubes) and asked to identify differences and similarities between particular specimens. Up to four differences and five similarities were to be reported.

In the marking of this exercise, one mark was awarded for each 'correct' or 'acceptable' difference or similarity, respectively, reported by a pupil, up to a total of four marks for the differences and five for the similarities. In relation to the question of whether a reported difference is 'acceptable' or not, the APU scheme suggests that, for the award of a mark, the answer has to indicate how the two specimens are different. A simple answer of the type 'different shapes' would not be acceptable.

Process-related Assessment Criteria

Whenever the assessment of students' practical abilities and skills is to be based on the direct observation of their actions and activities, process-related performance criteria are required. In the majority of instances, assessments using a direct observation technique are appropriate only for judging manipulative skills and competences. Most other factors of practical ability, e.g. observational competence and the ability to plan investigations and to interpret experimental results, require outcome-based criteria for their assessment. Therefore, in this discussion, the focus will exclusively be on the assessment of manipulative skills.

In the simplest case, the performance features summarised in Table 5.2 can be adopted as criteria for assessing the various components of manipulative skills. However, any assessment based on them directly, i.e. without further refinement and elaboration, is likely to be impressionistic only, since the assessor can do little more than provide an intuitive and subjective judgement about most of the component skills. For more objective and, hence, reliable assessments, the broad performance features in Table 5.2 have to be 'operationalised'. This requires, in the first instance, that they are elaborated in relation to the practical task that is to be assessed.

An early attempt to transform generalised performance features into operational schemes for the assessment of manipulative skills was made by Eglen and Kempa and is illustrated by the following example.[11] The practical task in question is the preparation of 250 cm^3 of a standard solution of EDTA (ethylenediaminetetra-acetic acid) from a previously weighed quantity of the chemical. The part-assessment referred to here covered the two major stages of the operation, viz.

i The dissolving of the EDTA sample in water to give a concentrated solution.
ii The quantitative transfer of this solution to a volumetric flask and the dilution to the required volume.

Two versions of an assessment schedule were developed for this task. Both are shown in Table 5.3. In the first version, the generalised performance criteria in Table 5.2 are amplified by a range of possible performance points that may be considered in the assessment. In the second, a 'check-list' of specific performance criteria is presented in the form of single questions asking for Yes or No answers. A Yes response would indicate, in each case, satisfactory achievement of a performance criterior, whilst a No answer implies the opposite.

It is of interest to review briefly the main findings reported by Eglen and Kempa concerning the use of their assessment schedules. These are based on the information collected from 100 different teachers who were involved in the assessment of students' practical skills, using unelaborated general criteria only. Two conclusions are noteworthy:

i The more detailed and operationalised the performance criteria, the more objective is the assessment. This objectivity manifests itself in the degree of concordance found in the grades awarded by different teachers assessing the same students' performances. The use of only generalised performance criteria leads to highly discordant assessments, chiefly because of the adoption, by teachers, of widely differing performance features.
ii Assessments arrived at by check-list-type schedules give rise to higher grades or marks than those obtained from the other schedules. The reason for this is that, in the absence of criteria that require both positive and negative performance features to be considered, teachers tend to base their assessments chiefly on negative performance characteristics. The assessment then becomes a 'penalising' procedure in which marks or grades tend to be successively reduced if a student fails to perform in the correct or expected manner. The severity of the 'penalty' imposed for a particular shortcoming in performance can vary significantly from teacher to teacher.

Table 5.3. Two versions of a process-related assessment schedule

I. *Version identifying possible performance points*

(a) *Methodical working*   Grade

 e.g. *in the washing of glassware; in the transfer of solid and of solution; in the processes of rinsing and diluting; in the stirring and dissolving operations.*

 Features in the student's performance used for the grading.

_____

_____

(b) Experimental technique   Grade

 e.g. *that used in the handling of glassware and of materials; in the operations of dissolving, transfer, washing and dilution.*

 Features in the student's performance used for grading.

_____

_____

(c) Manual dexterity   Grade

 e.g. *in the general manner of performance and in the completion of the task.*

 Features in the student's performance used for the grading.

_____

_____

(d) Orderliness   Grade

 e.g. *in the utilisation of bench-space and the organisation of equipment.*

 Features in the student's performance used for the grading.

_____

_____

Section A – Dissolution of the solid in water

a.1. Were the beaker and the stirring rod initially washed with distilled water?

Yes ☐ No ☐

a.2. After the transfer of the solid into the beaker, was the weighing bottle rinsed out with water?

Yes ☐ No ☐

a.3. Was the addition of water to the solid in the beaker done carefully, i.e. down the side of the beaker?

Yes ☐ No ☐

a.4. Was the solution stirred until all the solid had dissolved?

Yes ☐ No ☐

b.1. Was the beaker containing the solution adequately supported during stirring?

Yes ☐ No ☐

b.2. Was the stirring action itself safe and satisfactory?

Yes ☐ No ☐

b.3. Were all operations carried out in a manner which did not conflict with the quantitative nature of the exercise?

Yes ☐ No ☐

Section B – Transfer and dilution of the solution

a.1. Was the overall working sequence during the transfer of the solution from the beaker into the volumetric flask logical and acceptable?

Yes ☐ No ☐

a.2. Was all glassware washed with distilled water, prior to use?

Yes ☐ No ☐

a.3. Was a funnel used when transferring the solution from the beaker to the flask?

Yes ☐ No ☐

a.4. Was the solution remaining in the beaker rinsed over into the flask?

Yes ☐ No ☐

a.5. Was the solution adhering to the funnel washed down prior to its removal?

Yes ☐ No ☐

a.6. Were all rinsing operations carried out more than once?

Yes ☐ No ☐

a.7. Was the dilution of the solution in the flask effected in two stages?

Yes ☐ No ☐

	Yes	No
a.8. Was the solution shaken before the final 'topping-up' of the solution in the flask?	☐	☐
b.1. When pouring the solution from the beaker into the funnel, did the student use a glass rod?	☐	☐
b.2. Was the meniscus at eye-level during the 'topping-up' procedure?	☐	☐
b.3. Was the shaking procedure adequate?	☐	☐
c.1. Was the overall procedure carried out confidently and without undue hesitation?	☐	☐
c.2. Did the actions indicate that the student was at all times aware of the quantitative nature of the experiment?	☐	☐
c.3. Was the overall process carried out without 'mishaps'?	☐	☐
d.1. Was the working area maintained in a reasonable state of order throughout the experiment?	☐	☐
d.2. Was apparatus no longer in use removed from the immediate working area?	☐	☐

These findings confirm the importance of the use by teachers of assessment procedures that are based on fairly precisely formulated performance criteria, if reliable and comparable assessments are to be made. The use of check-list type schedules offers the best solution in this respect, although their development can be difficult and is usually time-consuming. Assessments based solely on generalised performance criteria are likely to lack both validity and reliability and should be avoided.

In the course of their investigations into pupils' ability to 'perform investigations', the APU Science teams have made extensive use of the check-list mode of assessment, not only for the assessment of manipulative actions performed by the pupils but also of the experimental conditions employed by them in particular investigations. Detailed information about this can be found in the relevant APU science publications.[12] Here, only one example is given, concerning an investigative task in which pupils are required to find out which of four kinds of environment woodlice prefer.

The particular environments to be investigated were damp and dark, dry and dark, damp and light, dry and light. Pupils were given a range of apparatus which they could use in the investigation, including foam bases, perspex frame, black plastic sheeting, brush and water, in addition to an adequate number of woodlice.

For the assessment of pupils' actions, the check-list shown in Fig. 5.2 was used. The actions of a particular pupil have been recorded on it. The entries show, for example, that the pupil carried out two separate trials, establishing two sets of conditions in each, and that, for each trial, from two to five woodlice were used. Further performance features can readily be deduced from the check-list and this demonstrates the general usefulness of check-lists for coding and assessment purposes.

It should be noted that not all the criteria that appear in the assessment check-list for the 'woodlice' experiment are process-related. As may be readily seen, those stated near the end of the schedule express the outcomes found in the various environments. Assessment schedules developed for other APU experiments likewise tend to combine process- and outcome-related criteria, thus indicating that the two types of criterion can readily co-exist in operational assessment check-lists.

Fig. 5.2 Check-list for assessment of 'woodlice' investigation.

Source: cf. ***DES Science in Schools Age 15: Report No. 2*** **Department of Education and Science HMSO (London) 1984.**

This checklist indicates that the pupil undertook two trials.

In the first trial, half the frame was dry and dark and the other half was dry and light. The pupil had used card to cover the top of the frame and plastic for the sides, enabling darkness to be achieved at one end.

Four woodlice were used; they were put into the centre of the frame by hand.

After waiting 90 seconds (not timed by pupil) the number of woodlice in each environment was counted.

In the second trial, half the frame was damp and light and half was dry and light. The water was applied evenly.

No new lice were added to the frame – the same lice were left for a further 70 seconds and again the number in each condition was counted.

									1	2	3	4
KEY		**CONDITIONS**										
DAMP ~												
DARK ‖‖‖												

		1	2	3	4
	Conditions set up – damp-light		1		
	– damp-dark				
	– dry-light	1	1		
	– dry-dark	1			
	approx. equal area for each condition	1	1		
WATER	Applied water – evenly		1		
	– with standing water				
	– on top of woodlice				
COVER	Used roof cover – card	1			
	– plastic				
	Used side cover – card				
	– plastic	1			
	Darkness achieved	1			
FLOOR	Darkened floor – card				
	–plastic				
WOODLICE	Used new selection of lice	1			
	Transferred them – by brush				
	– fingers	1			
	– 'tip and push'				
	Placed them in centre	1			
	Interfered with lice during trial				
	Number of lice used 1				
	2–5	1	1		
	More than 5				
	Actual number used	4	4		
TIME	Started clock				
	Noted time in each condition				
	Waited over 60s	1			
	Waited until lice stopped				
	Actual time	90s	70s		
	Counted number in each condition	1	1		
	Recounted after further time lapse				
	at regular intervals				
	Actual % of damp-light/whole				
	damp-dark/whole				
	dry-light/whole				
	dry-dark/whole				
	Trial/s used in record to conclude				
	Approach used in each trial with record				

Converting Assessments into Grades

Normally, the desired end-product of an assessment is some mark or grade that expresses a student's performance relative either to the performances of other students on the same task (norm-referencing) or to some set of 'external' performance criteria (criterion-referencing). For this to be achieved, the raw data derived immediately from an assessment, especially if they are based on the use of check-lists, need to be transformed into marks or grades. In this section, the principles underlying this process are briefly considered.

In the event that the final marks or grades are to be *norm-referenced*, the first step in the conversion of assessment data into grades consists of placing all students in a rank order. This can then be followed by the imposition of some grade distribution on this rank order. An example of this is given in Table 5.4, which is based on a recommendation made by the Joint Matriculation Board (JMB) for its A-level Physics examination.

Table 5.4. **Example of norm-referenced grade distribution**

Grade to be awarded	Grade description	Percentages of candidates in grade category
5	Best candidates	5–10
4	Better than avarage candidates	15–25
3	Average candidates	30–45
2	Worse than average candidates	15–25
1	Worst candidates	5–10

In the JMB procedure, the notion of the 'average candidate' is of central importance for it is used as the reference against which the performances of other candidates are judged. No doubt, the adoption of this reference simplifies the grading task that an individual teacher has to accomplish. However, it also poses problems concerning the comparability of the grades awarded by different teachers. These will be discussed in the following section on the moderation of practical grades.

The procedure for the translation of assessment results into *criterion-referenced* grades again involves two basic steps but these are different from those described for the norm-references procedure. The first, very essential, step consists of the description of different grades in terms of performance or achievements that are deemed appropriate to each grade. Students' actual performances, observed or recorded during an assessment, can then be compared with these grade descriptions and hence graded.

Table 5.5 gives two examples of sets of grade descriptions developed for a five-point grading scale. The grade descriptions relate to students' abilities to organise practical work and follow instructions and to the

Table 5.5. Example of criterion-based grade descriptions

Grade to be awarded	Ability/skill to be assessed	
	Ability to organise practical work and follow instructions	Accuracy of observations and measurements
5	Student has a clear understanding of the purpose of the experiment. He is able to organise the work in a safe and logical manner, in accordance with instructions provided.	Student observes, measures and records accurately and with due care.
4	Student requires some help to understand the aim of the experiment. He is able to follow the instruction, but needs some help to develop a safe and logical working procedure on their basis.	Observations, measurements are generally satisfactory, but may be subject to errors in precision or recording.
3	Student requires considerable help to understand the purpose of the experiment and to organise his work; he is able to follow instructions only if given a significant amount of assistance.	Student fails to exercise proper care in observations and measurements; some observations are missed and measurements lack in accuracy. Errors in recording.
2	Student has to rely on much help and support to be able to understand the aims of the work and to organise it. Help is needed even with simple instructions.	Significant inaccuracies in observations and measurements. Many observations either not made or not recorded.
1	No understanding of the aim of the experiment and its organisation is shown, even with help. Student is unable to follow instructions.	Observations and measurements are generally incorrect or unreliable or are not noted.

accuracy of their observations and measurements, respectively. Sets of grade descriptions for other areas of practical work in science have recently been developed for a number of GCSE science syllabuses, and the reader is referred to these.

The Moderation of Practical Grades

As was pointed out above, the most reliable assessments of students' practical skills result from the use of detailed check-lists specifying precise performance criteria. However, even if such check-lists are employed by teachers, this does not guarantee that their assessments are made to a 'common standard' that would ensure a high comparability of grades derived from them. On the contrary, as Eglen and Kempa found in their 1974 study,[13] the grades awarded by teachers assessing given (video-recorded) practical performances using detailed check-lists showed discrepancies from the respective mean grades by up to a full grade point on a five-point grading scheme.

In practice, it is impossible for teachers to operate to a common standard when making assessments. Even if external guidance is provided about grading standards, for example by an examinations board, the individual teacher will have to interpret the information received in the light of personal experience and perception. Thus, inter-teacher variability of assessments made and grades derived from them is inevitable.

Normally, inter-teacher or inter-school variability of grades is of little importance. For example, there is no reason why the end-of-year grades awarded to pupils in one school should conform to the same standard as those awarded in another school. However, if school- or teacher-based assessments are to be merged with external examination results, as is the case for several GCE A-level science examinations, it is important that grades awarded by different teachers or schools are so adjusted or 'moderated' that they conform to a common standard. Since this common standard must apply to the *totality* of the examined population, it has to be defined externally by an examining board. Individual teachers cannot, of course, be precisely aware of this common standard and are thus not able to place their students accurately on the overall scale of ability as it applies to the whole population of examinees.

The likely result of this is that a teacher may either *over-* or *under-* assess his students relative to the total examined population. A further possibility is that the teacher uses grade intervals that, when compared with those applied to the totality of candidates, may be either too wide or too narrow. If the former is the case, the spread of grades awarded by him will be greater than it should be; in the latter case, 'grade bunching' results.

The function of a moderating procedure is to detect and then to elimi-nate, or at least reduce, any over- or under-assessment to which teacher assessments of practical skills may be subject and, at the same time, correct any undue dispersion of grades within a teaching set. Three different approaches to the moderation of practical grades have been suggested. These are:

- moderation via the inspection of students' notebooks and written records of practical work,
- use of visiting moderators,
- statistical moderation of teacher-based grades.

In the following, these three procedures are described and evaluated.

Inspection of Practical Notebooks, etc.

In this procedure, schools are required to submit to an examining board candidates' practical notebooks and other records of practical work undertaken by them during their course. These are then scrutinised by the board's examiners and assessed in terms of the range and quality of the practical work carried out by the students. On the basis of these assessments, the 'level' of the examination entry of a school is gauged and this may be followed by adjustments to the candidates' practical grades.

The basic assumption underlying this approach to moderation is that the quality of candidates' written laboratory reports represents a valid measure of their actual practical abilities. Little evidence exists in support of this assumption; on the contrary, most studies reported in the literature point to a low correlation between the two qualities. Thus, this particular method of moderation must be viewed with considerable re-servation.

Moderation by Visiting Moderators

This procedure involves the assessment, by an external examiner or moderator, of the quality of students' practical work carried out in the course of an actual laboratory session. The moderator's assessment can subsequently be compared with the grades awarded by the teacher and appropriate adjustments made to the latter.

Apart from the direct moderation of a teacher's grading, the moderator can, through advice to the teacher, have a direct influence upon the experimental work organised by the teacher and his or her standard of assessment. This must be rated as a distinct advantage of this approach to moderation, although this is counterbalanced by the high costs (manpower and time) associated with it. Also, if several moderators are involved in the large-scale application of this method, problems of varia-bility in judgement between moderators may arise.

Statistical Moderating Procedures

The fundamental issue in the development of a statistical moderating procedure is to find some instrument or measure by which the extent of a teacher's over- or under-assessment of his students, relative to the total examined population, can be determined. It is natural, if only for reasons of administrative convenience, to look towards paper-and-pencil tests for this purpose. Current practice of the examination boards is to use students' overall results on the compulsory components of theory examinations (usually a multiple-choice and a structured paper, neither of which allows a choice of questions) as the 'external' measure with which to compare teacher-based grades for practical work. Earlier attempts involved the use of theory questions specifically concerned with aspects of practical work, but this had no significant advantage over the present procedure.

The choice of a theory examination as a reference standard for the moderation of practical grades is not beyond criticism. The major point of criticism is implied in the question of whether any significant relationship can be assumed to exist between students' practical abilities and their theoretical knowledge, even if this relates to practical situations. From a strictly theoretical point of view, there does not seem to be any *a priori* justification for this assumption. However, it must be remembered that 'practical abilities', as defined in the context of teacher assessment, go beyond purely manipulative and observational skills and also encompass facets that have a strong theoretical bias, viz. interpretation and planning abilities. This provides at least some justification for the use of theory marks as a measure against which to moderate practical grades.

Evidence in support of the latter point was reported by Futcher, who studied the relationship among teachers' assessments of their students' abilities in the manipulative, observational, interpretive and planning areas, respectively, and also compared these assessments with the marks obtained by these students in the compulsory part of their A-level theory examination as well as in their external practical examination.[14] The data are summarised in Table 5.6.

In relation to the issue under discussion here, two points are noteworthy. First, a moderately high interrelationship is seen to exist between all qualities covered by the teacher assessment. Thus, the use of an aggregate 'total' (M + O + I + P; see Table 5.6) to represent the component skills is entirely justified. Secondly, it is noted that the correlation between teacher-derived total scores and students' theory marks is moderately high ($r = 0.59$), indicating that the use of theory marks for moderating purposes is not unjustified. Indeed, it must be stressed that teacher-based grades correlate far more strongly with theory marks than

Table 5.6. Correlation between teacher-based and 'external' assessments in A-level Chemistry

	M	O	I	P	Total
Teacher-based assessments					
Manipulative skills (M)	—				
Observational skills (O)	0.56	—			
Interpretation abilities (I)	0.49	0.61	—		
Planning abilities (P)	0.49	0.56	0.61	—	
Total (M + O + I + P)	0.73	0.78	0.83	0.80	
'External' examination marks					
Theory paper (compulsory parts)	0.34	0.45	0.57	0.49	0.59
External practical examination	0.24	0.28	0.27	0.26	0.33

with external practical examination grades.

The moderation itself involves the application of statistical procedures, at least for large and moderately sized teaching sets (small teaching sets of, say, three or fewer students cannot be treated by statistical means). Most of these statistical procedures are based on the following rationale:

i The position of a given teaching set relative to the positions of all other teaching sets covered by the examination should be the same for both the theory and the practical assessment.
ii The spread of practical grades within a teaching set should reflect the spread of theory marks for that set, relative to the spread of those marks observed for the total examined population.

A further principle frequently stipulated is that a moderating procedure should not affect the rank order of candidates within a teaching set. This is in accord with the primary function of the moderation, which is to eliminate the effects of teachers' assessment characteristics.

Most procedures employed for the statistical moderation of teachers' grades are based on the notion of 'linear scaling', which is amply described in textbooks on statistics. The following equations illustrate the procedure:

$$\bar{G}_j \,(\text{mod}) = \bar{\bar{G}} + (\bar{T}_j - \bar{\bar{T}})\, \bar{S}_G / \bar{S}_T$$

$$S_j \,(\text{mod}) = S_T \times \bar{S}_G / \bar{S}_T$$

where: $\bar{G}_j$ (mod) = mean practical grade of teaching set j, after moderation; $\bar{G}$ = average of mean practical grades for all teaching sets; $\bar{T}_j$ =
mean theory mark of teaching set j, derived from theory examination;
$\bar{\bar{T}}$ = average of mean theory marks, for all teaching sets; S_j(mod) =
adjusted standard deviation of practical grades for teaching set j, following moderation; S_T = standard deviation of theory marks for set j; $\bar{S}_G$ =
mean of standard deviations of practical grades within sets, for all sets;
$\bar{S}_T$ = mean of standard deviations of theory marks within sets, for all
sets. Between them, the two equations adjust the mean and the spread of
the practical grades awarded by a teacher for teaching set j.

The moderated practical grade of an individual i in teaching set j, can
thus be obtained from his or her raw grade, G_{ij}, using the equation

$$G_{ij}(\text{mod}) = G_j(\text{mod}) + (G_{ij} - \bar{\bar{G}})\, S_j(\text{mod})\, /\bar{S}_G$$

To illustrate the application of the above equations, consider the
following figures derived from a study by Slimming.[15] In this, teacher
assessments of practical abilities were compared with students' performances on a paper-and-pencil test. The teacher assessments were made
on a five-point scale and, for some 30 teaching sets, gave a mean set grade
for all teaching sets of 3.0, with a standard deviation of 0.7. Correspond-
ingly, the theory test produced a mean set mark of 49.0%, with a standard
deviation of 11.0%. In accordance with the rationale outlined above, the
following correspondences should thus apply:

Mean theory mark for teaching set (%)	Mean practical grade for set
27.0	1.6
38.0	2.3
49.0	3.0
60.0	3.7
71.0	4.4

Note that, in each case, the mark or grade interval represents one standard deviation.

The actual effect of the moderation process on mean test grades can be
seen from the data for two teaching sets chosen here to exemplify cases of
over-assessment and under-assessment, respectively.

It is seen that, in the case of School A, the mean practical grade arrived
at by the teacher is too high compared with the set's theory performance.
Hence, the moderation reduces this mean grade to 2.7. In the case of
School B, the situation is reversed and an upward scaling of the mean
grade is indicated.

School	Teacher-derived practical grade (mean)	Theory score (mean)	Moderated practical grade (mean)
A	3.56	44.4	2.7
B	2.71	59.2	3.7

Adjustments made to mean grades for teaching sets will ultimately affect the grades of individual students also. Thus, in the case of School A, an original grade of 4 would be reduced to 3.4; whereas in the other case, it would be enhanced to 4.6. However, such adjustments appear to be entirely meaningful and justifiable.

As already suggested, statistical moderating procedures cannot satisfactorily be applied for the moderation of practical grades of small teaching sets. The examining boards are fully aware of this and, for teaching sets of less than four students or so, they rely on methods of 'visual inspection of grades' in order to avoid gross inconsistencies between candidates' theory marks and school-based practical grades.

Conclusion

In this chapter, the discussion has centred on a range of issues concerned directly or indirectly with the assessment of students' practical abilities in science. A distinction was made between outcome- and process-related assessments and the argument advanced that the latter might well be preferable in the context of school science education.

For a valid and reliable assessment of students' manipulative skills (as opposed to their observational, interpretative and planning abilities), the use of direct observation techniques is indispensable, but these have to be based on carefully developed assessment schedules. Detailed check-lists of performance criteria are particularly useful here, and several examples of such lists have been given.

Although the widespread adoption of schemes of teacher assessment of practical abilities has to be welcomed for educational reasons, it cannot be denied that this can give rise to problems both for the examining boards and for the teachers carrying out assessments. Problems affecting the examining boards are mainly concerned with the effective moderation of teachers' assessments, prior to their incorporation into formal examination grades. Problems faced by teachers tend to be of a different kind and relate mainly to the practical implementation of schemes of internal assessment. Many of these have so far received only little attention, either in development work or in research; yet they require solutions if teacher involvement in the assessment of practical abilities is to become a widely accepted feature of our examination structure.

Finally, it must be pointed out that 'attitudes towards practical work' are often included among the practical abilities to be assessed in students. No mention has been made here of the assessment of attitudes, for the simple reason that it is logically inconsistent to regard attitudes as a component of students' practical skills (or intellectual abilities, for that matter). Therefore, the assessment of attitudes is dealt with separately, in the next chapter.

Notes and References

1 See, for example L.C. Comber and J.P. Keeves *Science Education in Nineteen Countries* Halsted Press (New York) 1975.

2 See *Notes on Teacher-based Assessment of Practical Work in Chemistry* issued by the University of London Examinations Department.

3 J.R. Eglen and R.F. Kempa 'Assessing manipulative skills in practical chemistry.' *School Science Review*, Volume 56 pages 261–273.

4 Department of Education and Science (DES) *Practical Testing at Ages 11, 13 and 15. APU Science Report for Teachers No. 6* Department of Education and Science (London) 1985.

5 J.G. Buckley 'Investigation into assessment of practical abilities in sixth-form chemistry courses.' M.Sc. thesis (University of East Anglia) 1970.

6 R.F. Kempa 'Teacher assessment of practical skills in chemistry' in D.E. Hoare, R.F. Kempa and P.A. Ongley *Research in Assessment II* The Chemical Society [now Royal Society of Chemistry] Assessment Group (London) 1979 pages 15–26.

7 R.A. Chalmers and J. Stark 'Continuous assessment of practical work in the Scottish HNC Course in Chemistry.' *Education in Chemistry*, Volume 5 (1968) page 154.

8 DES *Science in Schools. Age 15: Report No. 2* Department of Education and Science (London) 1984.

9 J.E. Ward 'A study of observational attainment in practical work in school chemistry.' Ph.D. thesis (University of Keele) 1981.

10 DES *Science in Schools. Age 13: Report No. 2* Department of Education and Science (London) 1984.

11 J.R. Eglen and R.F. Kempa, see note 3 above.

12 See, for example, DES *Science in Schools*, notes 8 and 10 above. Additional information is given in other volumes of the DES *Science in Schools* series, in which the results of the APU science monitoring work are described.

13 J.R. Eglen and R.F. Kempa, see note 3 above.

14 D.A. Futcher 'An investigation into the moderation of teachers' assessments of sixth-form practical chemistry.' M.Sc. thesis (University of East Anglia) 1973.

15 D. Slimming 'Investigation into some aspects of teacher-based assessment of sixth-form chemistry students' interpretational abilities.' M.Sc. thesis (University of East Anglia) 1971.

6

The Assessment of Attitudes and Other Affective Characteristics

As was pointed out in Chapter 1, science curriculum projects and examination syllabuses frequently call for qualities to be developed in students, that fall outside the broad domains of intellectual abilities and experimental skills. Generally, these qualities relate to the development of students' interests in, and attitudes towards, science and the study of science, but sometimes touch upon other facets, e.g. the students' personal beliefs, values and even social skills. The following statements, all taken or adapted from actual science curricula or syllabuses, exemplify this.

Students should

- develop a lasting interest in science and concern for the application of scientific knowledge within the community;
- develop satisfactory attitudes towards safety regulations and exercise care in the execution of laboratory tasks;
- display honesty and integrity in the communication of scientific observations and data;
- be sceptical towards suggested (scientific) theories and explanations, yet willing to search for and test scientific hypotheses and theories;
- develop the ability to work in groups and as members of a team.

Qualities expressed or implicit in these statements are generally referred to as 'affective' qualities, to distinguish them from cognitive (= intellectual) and from psychomotor (= experimental, manipulative) skills and abilities. However, this distinction should not be interpreted as implying that affective aspects of behaviour can be rigorously separated from cognitive and/or psychomotor ones. On the contrary, qualities from the three areas frequently overlap. For example, a student's adherence to certain safety standards in laboratory work or other practical activities is bound to have its origin in an understanding of the principles of safety. Similarly, acceptance or rejection, as the case may be, of certain values stems frequently from an appraisal and evaluation of arguments and counter-arguments rooted in cognitive foundations, not merely emotional ones.

The Assessability of Affective Characteristics

Despite the emphasis that is often placed on the development in students of positive attitudes and other affective characteristics, attempts to assess these qualities are very rare. Certainly, the majority of public examinations concentrate on the assessment of students' attainment in the cognitive and psychomotor domain and bypass completely the affective domain.

The question must be asked, why should this be so; why have examining boards and curriculum development groups, for example, done so little to develop and promote the assessment of students' affective qualities and achievements?

There are at least two answers to this question, both to do with the *assessability* of affective characteristics, though seen from different perspectives. The first concerns the technical and methodological difficulties that are associated with the assessment of affective qualities; the second relates to some ethical issues that can arise in connection with the assessment of certain affective characteristics. Both give rise to the question of whether and to what extent it is possible, for technical or ethical reasons, to engage in assessment of students' attitudes and related qualities.

Some Technical and Methodological Problems

Practically all statements found in curriculum publications and examination syllabuses to describe the affective qualities to be developed by students are couched in terms that convey an impression of the broad nature of these qualities, but fail to give precise elaborations of ways in which they might manifest themselves in students' overt behaviour. The lack of such elaborations immediately poses a major problem for those wishing to assess students' affective characteristics. The problem concerns the translation of the broad, global statements about affective qualities into operationally meaningful criteria that can be assessed more or less objectively and from which the absence or presence of certain affective characteristics may be inferred. Without this translation, affective qualities stated loosely as part of a set of educational intentions cannot be assessed and so would serve no function other than that of 'window-dressing'.

Some examples of the results of such translation exercises are given further on in this chapter. But, as will be seen, they relate to 'straightforward' attitudinal characteristics only, for which the specification of operational assessment criteria is relatively simple: e.g. 'attitudes towards safety procedures' or 'perseverance in the performance of laboratory investigations'. Other affective qualities are more difficult to define operationally, as 'critical attitude of mind', for example, and this clearly affects their assessability. An additional problem here is that often no consensus exists among curriculum workers, examiners and teachers about the specific behaviours and traits that can be associated with particular broadly defined affective qualities. Gardner, in a well-written critique of attitude testing in science education, discusses this issue in detail.[1]

The major source of the difficulties that we encounter in the assessment of attitudes and other affective characteristics is the existence of these qualities *within* individuals: they cannot be seen, felt or observed in any direct way. In this respect, affective qualities differ fundamentally from cognitive and psychomotor skills: the latter can be associated with definite outcomes and achievements that are open to overt assessment. By contrast, for the assessment of attitudes, etc., we rely on observing a student's response to some event or situation, and it is from the nature of the response that we *infer* his or her attitude. The response made by the student does, of course, have to be observed and interpreted by the assessor and this immediately introduces a subjective note into the assessment of affective qualities. As a result, the validity and reliability with which it is possible to measure affective variables are generally significantly lower than for cognitive and psychomotor variables.

The Ethical Perspective

Some of the affective qualities to which reference is made in curricula and syllabuses lie within, or close to, the personality and character domain of human traits. For example, working habits and preferences (i.e. whether a student prefers to work individually or in a group) would seem to constitute an aspect of an individual's personality and can hardly be considered to be the outcome of the educational process to which the student is or was exposed. Likewise, certain values and attitudes, e.g. in relation to social and moral issues, may well be the result of influences emanating from the student's home environment. In these and similar instances, an important question arises: to what extent, if at all, can the assessment of these qualities form a legitimate part of the assessment of a student's affective characteristics?

There is no ready-made answer to this question. One may pursue the issue further by asking whether one can, in fact, establish a clear correspondence between affective characteristics as they may be apparent in students, and the nature of the curriculum and the teaching to which they were exposed. Judging from numerous research studies, this correspondence appears to be weak and dubious: little, if any, causal relationship would seem to exist between students' values and attitudes and *formal* educational influences. This finding should not surprise us, for the simple reason that few of the instructional practices found in science education (and elsewhere) are directly oriented towards affective goals. Indeed, our knowledge about how attitudinal and value changes may be brought about through educational interventions is still rather scant.

If it is accepted that many attitudes and values that may develop in the learner cannot be directly attributed to curriculum influences, any suggestion that such qualities should be assessed must be a questionable proposition. In other words, the matter of the assessability of affective characteristics arises again, but this time from the ethics point of view. To resolve this issue, it is suggested that the assessment of students' affective characteristics can be justified in two circumstances:

i When the affective characteristic can be attributed directly to curriculum influences. In general, these characteristics are associated with particular subjects (for example, the sciences) and invariably incorporate substantial cognitive elements.
ii Where the affective characteristic relates directly to, or has a significant bearing on, the way in which a student performs in an academic task, or where the success in the task may be dependent on the characteristic.

On the grounds of these criteria, the assessment of most of the affective qualities that relate to practical work in the sciences is readily justified. For example, a student's 'resourcefulness' in the conduct of experimental work may be thought of as a characteristic qualifying under (i): resourcefulness presupposes a sound understanding of an experimental problem and an awareness of ways and techniques that may be applied to solve it. Likewise, 'perseverance in designing and performing experiments' may also be regarded as a legitimate quality for assessment, in accordance with criterion (ii).

Techniques for the Assessment of Affective Characteristics

Techniques for the measurement of attitudes and other affective qualities fall broadly into three categories:

1 Interviews, either 'open-ended' or 'structured', between student and assessor; these can be held in formal or informal settings.
2 Written tests and inventories of varying types; in the main these are used for attitude and interest measurement.
3 Direct observation of students in situations that require the display of affective characteristics.

A detailed appraisal of these categories is beyond the scope of this chapter. However, some of the major advantages and disadvantages associated with each type of technique are outlined briefly in the following sections.

Interviewing Techniques

It has been said that an interview may be thought of as an 'oral question-naire' wherein the interviewer tries to obtain information about the interviewee. Through skilful questioning, the interviewer can explore an interviewee's responses and reaction to a range of different situations or propositions and, from there, gauge the latter's likes, dislikes, prejudices and attitudes. Interviews may be structured or unstructured. In the former, the content of the interview, and the sequence and formulation of questions are predetermined, so that a highly reproducible setting can be achieved for the interview. Unstructured interviews tend to be 'open-ended' in outcome: they are 'played by ear', without confinement to a predetermined set of questions. Indeed, answers given by an interviewee may form the starting point to new lines of questioning, depending on whether the interviewer considers these to be potentially fruitful.

The absence from open-ended, unstructured interviews of any form of standardised content or procedure causes any assessments made on their basis to be strongly subjective and of questionable validity and reliability. In contrast, structured interviews, which require the use of detailed interviewing schedules, give fairly objective information about, for example, students' attitudes and interests. However, in many cases structured interviews offer little advantage over written questionnaires or inventories, except that follow-up questions may be asked and ambiguities and misunderstandings corrected in situ.

Interviews, whether structured or unstructured, involve direct interactions between an interviewer and interviewee. It is widely recognised that in interactive situations the characteristics of the interviewer may have a significant effect upon the responses obtained from the interviewee. This may be the result of the interviewee misinterpreting or misperceiving the questions asked, or – and this has often been claimed – tailoring answers to what he or she believes to be desirable in the interviewer's view. Thus, it is not impossible for information derived from interviews to be significantly distorted!

Written Tests

Written tests cover a wide variety, from simple questionnaires and attitude surveys to sophisticated attitude and value inventories. Good (i.e. valid and reliable) tests and inventories are difficult to construct and require developmental procedures not unlike those used for multiple-choice tests.

In terms of content and structure, written tests resemble structured interviews, but are more convenient for large-scale administration. Like interviews, they have the disadvantage that the respondent can produce or select answers that may or may not correspond to his real attitudes. For example, a student may *claim* to have particular likes or preferences simply because he judges these to be desirable in the assessor's view. Thus, the responses given to an attitude test can be coloured by how the student interprets the purpose of the test. The danger of this happening is particularly pronounced in the case of simple, unsophisticated tests.

The main types of attitude test and inventory are exemplified and discussed further below.

Direct Observation

In the case of certain attitudinal characteristics, it is possible to infer their presence or absence directly from the behaviour of the student. For example, learners' attitudes towards safety requirements and rules are likely to manifest themselves in their actions in the laboratory. Likewise, students' perseverance in tackling a task can readily be judged from the way in which they address themselves to the task. Thus, direct observation becomes a further technique by which attitudinal qualities can be assessed.

It should be noted that not all attitudinal qualities lend themselves to assessment by direct observation. Qualities such as satisfaction, preference and likes/dislikes do not always manifest themselves in overt actions on the learner's part: rather, they refer to the inner state and disposition and may well be hidden.

Even when attitudes and other affective qualities are of a nature that renders them assessable by the direct observation technique, such assessments are usually far from straightforward, for two main reasons:

i The assessments are likely to be highly subjective and unreliable, unless they are based on clearly defined criteria. The identification of such criteria is, however, far more difficult than the specification of assessment criteria for the cognitive and psychomotor domains.

ii Teachers may not always be willing to engage in the assessment of qualities that, in their view, are 'non-academic' and/or that they do not feel qualified to judge.

A further difficulty associated with the assessment by teachers of their students' affective qualities is that, at least in the absence of detailed assessment criteria, such assessments are strongly influenced by teachers' knowledge and impressions of other characteristics exhibited by the learner, e.g. the quality of work and ability, as perceived by the teacher, as well as classroom behaviour. Evidence of this has been provided by, for example, Rickwood, who found fairly high correlations to exist between teachers' ratings of their pupils' attitudes to science, their personal application, classroom behaviour, interests and abilities and academic achievement in science (correlation coefficients ranged from 0.6 to 0.9).[2] In the light of these findings, Rickwood concluded:

The phenomenon of co-judgement is strongly in evidence . . . . After judging a pupil's academic performance or his classroom behaviour, it is usual (for teachers) to infer a commensurate level of interest and attitude towards the subject.

The foregoing comments about the three major techniques currently in existence for the assessment of attitudes and related characteristics, point clearly to the difficulties that we still encounter in reaching valid and reliable judgements about students' qualities in the affective domain. The main cause of these difficulties is the inadequate articulation, in operational terms, of the behaviour and responses on the part of students that may be deemed to be indicative of certain attitudes and other affective characteristics.

In the absence of detailed and meaningful assessment criteria, our judgements in this area are bound to be subjective and will lack reliability. Even if judgements made by individual teachers are acceptably consistent and reproducible, the comparability of grades for attitudes awarded by different assessors is likely to be low, far lower in fact than for assessments relating to qualities in the cognitive and the psychomotor domain.

The last point must obviously call into question the wisdom and propriety of including attitudes among the qualities to be judged by teachers as an aspect of their students' practical skills. This is not to say that development of positive attitudes to practical work is not a worthwhile educational aim – on the contrary, it is something that should be encouraged at all levels of science education. However, current assessment procedures do not allow teachers to assess these qualities in a valid and reliable way. Therefore, it may be argued, we should abandon the incorporation of attitude assessments into students' practical grades until better assessment techniques have been evolved.

The Assessment of Affective Characteristics in Practice

Actual attempts to measure attitudinal characteristics in science students fall broadly into two categories:

i Assessments made in connection with the teacher-based assessment of students' practical abilities.
ii Attitude measurements undertaken in the context of curriculum evaluation and science education researches.

Practising science teachers will normally be concerned only with attitude assessments falling into the first of these categories. Therefore, a fairly detailed discussion of these will be presented here. In relation to the second area of attitude measurements, the discussion will be restricted to some of the major types of inventory and questionnaire that have been successfully employed.

Assessing Attitudes towards Practical Work

Most examination boards operating schemes of teacher assessment of practical work require students' 'attitudes to practical work' to be assessed. The incorporation of attitudes into the range of qualities to be assessed by teachers can be traced back to the early days of the Nuffield A-level Chemistry examination, as has been described by Mathews:

In arriving at the objectives of the practical assessment, the teachers themselves were consulted and, as a result, attitudes to practical work were included . . . . Teachers are left with a good deal of freedom on how to arrive at this assessment, but observation of qualities such as willing co-operation with normal laboratory procedures, persistence in pursuing a practical problem even when difficulties arise, and enthusiasm for practical work as a worthwhile scientific pursuit, are suggested.[3]

It has to be admitted straightaway that the procedure advocated in this passage is so open-ended and lacking in operationality that it can hardly be expected to serve as the basis for valid and reliable assessments of students' attitudes to practical work. What it does though, and therein lies its merit, is to point to qualities to be considered to be an integral part of 'attitudes to practical work'. These are cooperation, persistence and enthusiasm.

In order to facilitate the assessment of attitudes by teachers, the GCE Boards have tended to recommend the use of rating scales, using descriptors like the following for a five-point scale:

5 Interested, eager and curious, enthusiastic, self-reliant and resourceful.
3 Moderately active in class and quite interested – gets on well with what he is told to do, but is not especially resourceful – persistent – needs interest to be stimulated.
1 Not interested at all – careless and unenthusiastic – passive in response – lacking in concentration – lackadaisical and diffident towards the subject.

The intermediate ratings of 4 and 2 would be appropriate for students whose behaviour is thought to fall between the descriptions given.

Rating scales like the foregoing have been successfully employed for a number of years now, although no information is available as to how reliable they have proved. It is reasonable to assume, though, that the assessments made by these means are not without variations due to subjectivity in judgements. These are likely to arise from two different factors: (i) inter-personal differences in the interpretation of phrases such as 'moderately active in class', and (ii) differences in the weighting given to the various 'features' listed in the descriptions of the scale points (these, it will have been noticed, incorporate different 'dimensions'). Notwithstanding these points, an adequate degree of consensus would normally be expected among the ratings by experienced teachers, and so the assessment of 'attitudes to practical work' comes within the scope of reasonable possibility.

Approaches to the Assessment of Attitudes to Science

Although attitude measurements have featured prominently in attempts at evaluating modern science curricula and related researches, the area of attitude assessment has remained one that is fraught with uncertainty and difficulties. There are two chief reasons for this:

i Inadequate consensus among evaluators and researchers about what constitutes 'attitudes' in the science education context, with the result that different workers have employed widely different definitions of 'attitudes towards science' or 'scientific attitudes'.
ii No 'standard' attitude tests or inventories are available so that, as a result, different workers have tended to develop their own 'home-made' instruments, frequently employing different techniques. The comparability of results and findings from such work cannot be assumed and, hence, it is often difficult to draw general conclusions from attitude measurement.

Rickwood has recently examined both these points and produced strong evidence in support of the assertions made here.[4] A construct analysis of over 50 attitude questionnaires published in the literature enabled him to identify at least 10 major science attitude 'dimensions' that different authors had sought to measure. These were:

- commitment and enjoyment of science;
- preference for scientific or science-related occupations;
- scientific interests and pastimes;
- characteristics of scientists;
- difficulty of science as a school subject;
- science and society;
- science and the individual;
- scientific theories and laws;
- the scientific method and processes of science;
- the aims of science.

Even a cursory glance at these titles[5] shows that some of the dimensions are rooted firmly in the cognitive area, for example how students see the scientific method or what they perceive to be the aims of science. But even when these particular dimensions are excluded, the remaining ones demonstrate the divergence in opinion about what constitutes attitudes to science. In the absence of an adequate agreement about this issue, it is not possible to design attitude tests and inventories to a 'common standard'. Whilst this does not invalidate the results obtained by means of individual tests, such results will in many instances relate to different attitude constructs and, hence, lack comparability. This is an important point ot be borne in mind when data on attitude, published in the literature, are considered.

The main approach to the assessment of students' attitudes towards science has been by means of written tests and inventories. Several well-established techniques are available for this purpose, among them:

(a) *Likert-type scaling*: this requires the students to indicate, for example, levels of agreement and disagreement with a particular statement, usually on a five-point rating scale.
(b) *The Semantic Differential technique*: in this the student has to choose a position between two opposing words or phrases describing an attitude.
(c) *Situational techniques*: here, a short story (the 'situation') is presented to the student, who is then required to express a reaction to it.

These techniques are illustrated and commented upon in the following sections.

(a) *Likert-type scaling*. The following three items exemplify this approach. In each case, students would be required to encircle one of the possible responses on the right that most closely reflects their feelings (AA denotes 'complete agreement', A = mild or partial agreement, N = undecided or neutral, D and DD denote mild/partial and complete disagreement, respectively).

1 Science discoveries that do not have a practical use
  are a waste of time.   AA   A   N   D   DD
2 Science has provided many helpful devices at home
  to make our lives easier.   AA   A   N   D   DD
3 I would rather do any other subject than science at
  school.   AA   A   N   D   DD

A full Likert-type inventory can comprise as many as 60 items, depending on the number of different attitude dimensions covered by it. For each dimension, between six and ten items are usually employed. A student's scores on these, translating the AA to DD into a 1–5 or 5–1 scale as appropriate, are aggregated into an overall score on the particular dimension.

(b) *Semantic Differential technique*. This is exemplified by the following items, each consisting of an expression and a rating scale. The latter is made up of descriptive, opposite word-pairs or phrases between which seven scale points are located. Students express their own responses or feelings by placing a cross (X) at the appropriate position of the scale.

1	Practical work in science	dull :	:	:	:	:	:	:	: exciting
2	Science in society	productive :	:	:	:	:	:	:	: wasteful
3	Working with a chemistry set	not enjoyable :	:	:	:	:	:	:	: enjoyable
4	Scientists in their work	disorganised :	:	:	:	:	:	:	: organised

Semantic differential items are generally simple and unsophisticated and do not allow complex attitudinal characteristics to be discerned or measured. The composition of a full test again depends on the number of attitude dimensions examined, but tests of between 60 and 80 items are not uncommon. The marking procedure adopted for semantic differential tests is similar to that for Likert-type inventories.

(c) *Situational techniques.* Two examples of situational items are given below. The first, developed by Hadden and Johnstone,[6] employs a rating procedure for its evaluation; the second, taken from a test by Rickwood and Kempa,[7] adopts an open-ended format of answering.

Example 1

(Designed to assess students' 'commitment to apply a scientific approach to other fields of experience'.)

A farmer noticed that, on gathering his crop of 'Golden Wonder' potatoes, the crop from one part of the field was very good, and that from the rest of the field was very poor. He suspected that the reason was that he had added two different types of artificial fertiliser to the soil at different parts of the field. He decided to investigate to try to prove his suspicions correct.

How important do you think each of the following would be in his investigations? Rate them on the following scale:

+3 must be done   +1 important   −2 very unimportant
+2 very important   −1 unimportant   −3 does not matter at all

	Rating
Check the average rainfall during the time the potatoes had grown	
Sow 'Golden Wonder' potatoes in two patches of soil, each treated with a different fertiliser and check the crop obtained	
Sow 'Golden Wonder' potatoes in soil with a third fertiliser and check the crop obtained	
Make sure that the original facts about the good and poor crops were correct	
Wait until next year's crop has been obtained from the same field before making the investigaton	
Analyse soil from several parts of the field to find what type of fertiliser has been added	
Plant a trial batch of 'Golden Wonders' deeper in the soil	
Analyse soil from several parts of the field to find how much fertiliser had been added	
Plant 'Kerr's Pinks' potatoes in the field and record the crop from various parts of the field	
Sow 'Golden Wonder' potatoes in soil containing no artificial fertiliser	
Check whether or not frost had occurred during the time the potatoes had grown	

Example 2

Jane and Mike were watching the news on television when it was announced that a large sum of money had been given to a new science project.

Jane said to Mike: 'I think that it is wrong to give science so much money. All that science does is to cause trouble and make a mess of the world.'

Mike had a different view and said: 'Well, I think that science should have as much money as it needs. Science helps us to solve all our problems today.'

Question: What do you think about science in our world?

Both types of item have been successfully employed in a number of studies of students' attitudes towards science, although neither is entirely free of problems. Items belonging to the first type are relatively easy to mark and evaluate, but have the disadvantage that students must respond to a predetermined range of responses, without being able to develop their own independent views. In the second item type, this problem is avoided but a different one arises, this time in connection with the evaluation of students' responses. These have to be carefully analysed and sorted into categories that can be meaningfully interpreted in terms of attitude traits. All in all, the nature of this task is such that one cannot recommend the use of this approach to attitudinal assessment outside the context of research.

Conclusion

There can be no doubt that, despite the considerable progress made over the past two decades in the development of valid and reliable assessment techniques, the assessment of students' affective and attitudinal characteristics has remained a problem issue. As has been indicated in this chapter, there are many reasons for this, in both the philosophical and technical sphere.

For the science teachers, this is perhaps not a satisfactory situation. On the one hand, the importance of affective aims and objectives is constantly brought to their attention, and this is coupled with an encouragement to use instructional procedures that promote the acquisition of positive attitudes to science. On the other hand, we still lack the techniques and tools whereby we can purposefully assess students' development and progress in this area.

The one exception to this is the assessment of 'attitudes to practical work', which is now a firmly established component of most schemes of teacher-assessment of practical abilities. The techniques developed for assessment in this area may lack some of the qualities, in terms of validity and reliability, that we have come to associate with assessment techniques for the cognitive and the psychomotor domain. Nevertheless, they have proved to be usable and useful.

Notes and References

1 P.L. Gardner 'Attitudes to science: a review.' *Studies in Science Education*, Volume 2 (1975) pages 1–41.

2 A.R. Rickwood 'Comparative evaluation of different methods for the assessment of attitudes to science.' Ph.D. thesis (University of Keele) 1984.

3 Nuffield Advanced Science *Examinations and Assessment* Penguin (Harmondsworth, Middlesex) 1972.

4 A.R. Rickwood, see note 2 above.

5 A.R. Rickwood (see note 2 above) has given a detailed description of these dimensions.

6 R.A. Hadden and A.H. Johnstone 'Affective objectives in the teaching of chemistry' in R. Kempa, D.E. Hoare and R.J.D. Rutherford *Research in Assessment* The Chemical Society [now Royal Society of Chemistry] (London) 1977 pages 18–24.

7 A.R. Rickwood and R.F. Kempa 'Reactions to science situations inventory.' Mimeographed document (University of Keele).

7

Towards Criterion-referencing in Examinations

Traditionally, most public examinations, e.g. those administered by the GCE Boards, have tended to be norm-referenced. This means that for the award of grades they rely extensively on the distribution of performances within an examination population and on the performance of candidates relative to one another, rather than on an evaluation of candidates' absolute attainments and abilities. The fact that the grade awarded to a candidate is dependent not only on the individual's performance, but also on that of other examinees, must be regarded as a serious shortcoming of current practice in public examinations.

In view of this situation, it is not surprising that considerable interest has been shown in recent years in the development and adoption, for public examinations, of criterion-referenced assessment procedures as an alternative to the current norm-referenced methods. The desirability of this move has been fully endorsed at the highest political level, as is evident from the following quote taken from an address by Sir Keith Joseph, Secretary of State for Education and Science, to the North of England Education Conference in Sheffield, on 6 January 1984. Referring to the new General Certificate of Secondary Examination (GCSE), to be introduced in 1988 to replace the current GCE O-level and CSE Examinations, he stated

we should move towards a greater degree of criterion-referencing . . . and away from norm-referencing. The existing system tells us a great deal about relative standards between candidates. It tells us much less about absolute standards. We lack clear definitions of the level of knowledge and performance expected from candidates for the award of particular grades.[1]

The major task in the development of an operational system of criterion-referenced assessment in the context of public examinations is to determine and specify the minimum levels of skills, abilities and attainment that have to be reached for a particular grade to be awarded. Once these minimum levels have been defined, they effectively become grade-related criteria. These can then be used to determine whether a candidate should be awarded one grade, rather than another.

Currently, in England, several projects are in progress that were specifically set up to develop grade-related criteria for use in the new GCSE examinations.[2] This work is carried out mainly under the auspices of some of the established examinations boards. In Scotland, it should be noted, a parallel development has taken place, under the auspices of the Scottish Examination Board, in relation to the new Scottish Standard Grade Examination.[3]

Until such time that the various projects in criterion-referencing (also referred to as Graded Assessment or Assessment of Graded Objectives) have published their findings and recommendations, it is not possible to give a full account of this development in our assessment and examining procedures. However, some preliminary information is available, and this is given in the following section. Thereafter, some of the technical difficulties associated with the introduction of a system of criterion-referenced examining are discussed.

Towards Meaningful Grade Descriptions

The main issue in the development of a criterion-referenced assessment scheme is the determination of what constitutes the minimum levels of attainment required for the award of a pass or a particular grade. Early attempts at describing performance criteria for certain grades in the new 16+ GCSE examination were made by the various Working Parties on 16+ National Criteria that were established in 1982 by a Joint Council set up by the GCE and CSE Boards. In the main, these descriptions referred to Grades C and F to be awarded under the new examination scheme.[4] Tables 7.1 to 7.4 give selected examples of these descriptions for biology, chemistry, physics and integrated science. For detailed information, the appropriate 16+ National Criteria documents should be consulted.[5]

Two points are noteworthy concerning the performance criteria given in the 16+ National Criteria documents. The first is that these criteria broadly reflect what members of the Working Parties perceived to be the typical minimum performances shown by students gaining the equivalent of the two grades in the current norm-referenced GCE/CSE examination system. Thus, they are essentially the result of attempts to adapt the existing population-related performance norms to a criterion-referenced examination structure. This relationship between the existing and the new system is, of course, very important: it ensures an acceptable degree of comparability between the two and, at the same time, defines the skills and competencies that may be associated with each grade.

The second point concerns the grade descriptions themselves. These vary widely not only in their specificity, but also in the extent to which

Table 7.1. Grade descriptions for Biology proposed by the 16+ National Criteria Working Party for Biology

Grade F	Grade C
Candidates achieving grade F are likely to be familiar with a sufficient body of facts to be able to understand a straightforward biological statement or problem, to be able to follow routine procedural instructions.	Candidates achieving grade C are likely to possess a cohesive body of facts sufficient to allow insight into the significance of a biological statement or problem and to be able to plan experiments and to draw conclusions.
More specifically, candidates are likely to demonstrate the ability	More specifically, candidates are likely to be able to demonstrate the ability
1 To recall basic biological facts and principles	1 To recall a wide range of biological facts and principles
2 To describe a limited range of simple biological experiments	2 To describe a wide range of biological experiments
3 To understand simple safety precautions in laboratory work	3 To understand simple safety precautions in laboratory work and explain the principles underlying them
4 To recall simple applications of biology in modern society	4 To recall simple applications of Biology in modern society and explain the principles underlying them
5 To make simple observations from a variety of sources (e.g. photographs, drawings, graphs)	5 To make accurate and detailed observations from a variety of sources (e.g. photographs, drawings, graphs)
6 To draw simple inferences from biological information	6 To analyse and interpret biological information
7 To use a knowledge of biological processes and principles in familiar situations	7 To use a knowledge of biological processes and principles in familiar situations and apply it to unfamiliar situations
8 To criticise the design of simple experiments	8 To criticise the design of simple experiments and suggest improvements
9 To use sufficient biological terms to avoid misunderstanding when communicating information	9 To use essential biological terms accurately when communicating information
10 To present biological information and ideas in a straightforward manner	10 To present biological information cogently in a variety of ways

Source: cf. DES GCSE (General Certificate of Secondary Education) –
The National Criteria (Biology) HMSO (London) 1985.

Table 7.2. Grade descriptions for Chemistry proposed by the 16+ National Criteria Working Party for Chemistry

Grade C

A minimum standard grade C candidate would be expected to demonstrate *considerable* competence in the assessment objectives in Category 1 (Knowledge), a *reasonable* competence in Category 2 (Comprehension) and *some* competence in Category 3 (Application, Analysis, Synthesis and Evaluation). A grade C candidate would also demonstrate *reasonable* competence in practical skills. For example, to be awarded grade C, a candidate should
  − show a good knowledge of factual chemistry;
  − show an understanding of the ideas of chemistry;
  − be able to write simple balanced chemical equations;
  − be able to examine data, find patterns and draw conclusions;
  − be able to perform numerical calculations in which the method of solution is specified;
  − be able to use chemical knowledge in everyday situations.

Grade F

A minimum standard grade F candidate would be expected to demonstrate a reasonable competence in the assessment of objectives in Category 1 (Knowledge), and some competence in Categories 2 (Comprehension) and 3 (Application, Analysis, Synthesis and Evaluation). Grade F candidates would also demonstrate some practical skills within Category 4 (Objectives for Practical Work). For example, to be awarded a grade F, candidates should
  − show some knowledge of factual chemistry;
  − be able to write word chemistry equations;
  − be able to plot simple graphs in which the axes are labelled.

Source: cf. DES GCSE *(General Certificate of Secondary Education)* – *The National Criteria (Chemistry)* HMSO (London) 1985.

Table 7.3. Examples of standards of attainment in various assessment areas in Physics, for grades C and F

Assessment objective	Expected performance level	
	Grade F	*Grade C*
Use of given formulae.	Use $v = f\lambda$ to calculate v, given values for λ and f.	Use $v = f\lambda$ to find any one of the variables, given the other two.

Explain phenomena in terms of models and theories.	Explain evaporation of a liquid.	Explain why evaporation produces cooling.
Design simple experiments.	Choose the means of measuring the diameter of a cylindrical object such as a test-tube.	Undertake the investigation of the relationship between the electrical energy used and the rise in temperature produced.
Extract information from that which is given.	Read data from a graph.	Determine the velocity from a displacement–time graph.
Recognise mistakes, misconceptions, unreliable data, and assumptions.	Recognition of a doubtful point on a straight-line graph.	Recognition of reasons for discrepancy between expected and actual results when water is heated and the temperature change is measured.
Draw conclusions and formulate generalisations.	Given a set of experimental data and a series of feasible conclusions or generalisations, student can recognise a likely conclusion and support this with a simple reason.	Given a set of experimental data, establish the proportionality between the quantities and draw an appropriate generalisation from the proportionality (e.g. Hooke's law).

Source: cf. DES GCSE (General Certificate of Secondary Education) –
The National Criteria (Physics) HMSO (London) 1985.

Table 7.4. Performance criteria for Grades C and F in relation to various science processes

Science process	Expected performance level	
	Grade F	Grade C
Observing	Notices things that are immediately apparent (possibly only with guidance) without being able to distinguish which observations are relevant to the task in hand. Records observations accurately.	Can see the significance of the observations made and can select information relevant to the task in hand.

Investigating	Can follow instructions, carry out a practical experiment and collect results satisfactorily.	Readily grasps the overall plan of practical enquiry, works through the stages competently and systematically, making appropriate decisions at each stage. Can suggest ways of testing explanations for patterns of observations. Can criticise the design of simple experiments.
Showing factual knowledge	Recalls scientific facts, laws, etc. Recognises terms. Obtains information from graphs, data, diagrams. Labels given diagrams correctly.	Assembles scientific facts, laws, etc. into logical sequence. Expresses information in the form of graphs. Constructs and labels diagrams correctly.
Searching for patterns	Can find straightforward patterns in information and observations or recognises them when guided.	Makes reasonable inferences that fit the evidence and attempts to explain patterns found in own observations. Can select and analyse information presented in a variety of ways.
Communicating	Can communicate information with sufficient clarity to be understood.	Organises and expresses ideas clearly using appropriate scientific terms, possibly showing evidence of wider reading.
Applying	Requires assistance to discriminate which information is applicable to new situations.	Can apply earlier learning to new situations by recognising relationships between one situation and another. Can use previous experience to relate 'school science' to wider issues but may need guidance.

Source: DES GCSE (General Certificate of Secondary Education) –
The National Criteria (Science) HMSO (London) 1985.

they are genuinely criterion-referenced. The chemistry descriptions in particular appear to be rather unsatisfactory in this respect: notions such as 'considerable', 'reasonable' or 'some', used to describe levels of competence, are in themselves highly ambiguous and are, at best, interpretable only in relation to the performance spectrum observed for the total examined population.

Grade descriptions developed for the new Scottish Standard Grade Examination are not unlike some of those given in Tables 7.1 to 7.4. For example, the summary grade-related criteria for Grade 5 Science in the Scottish scheme are as follows:

To be awarded this Grade a pupil has demonstrated ability to suggest and describe a procedure to solve a given problem, and to identify one of the factors which might affect the fairness of a scientific test. The pupil has shown ability to draw appropriate conclusions from data and make an attempt at explanations. In addition, the pupil has shown ability to draw valid conclusions from given information and suggest what might happen in related situations.[6]

It has to be stressed that grade descriptions like the foregoing and those in the tables can do little more than characterise the *typical* performance associated with a particular grade. Although they may well suffice for grading purposes when used by experienced examiners and assessors, they nevertheless require further elaboration in terms of specific subject matter items and competencies, if they are to be of use in normal classwork, e.g. as part of 'internal' assessments.

This elaboration forms part of the development work currently undertaken by the various projects on the assessment of graded objectives. To exemplify the likely outcome of such efforts, a range of skill items relating to the Interpretation and Application area and the Planning of Experiments area, respectively, is shown in Tables 7.5 and 7.6. These items are derived from a working document developed by the Science Curriculum Group of the Midland Examination Group's Project on Assessment of Graded Objectives. The particular items express 'core' science skill objectives of the kind that the majority of pupils taking a GCSE science course are expected to achieve. Assessment objectives for higher grade levels and other science skill areas are also being developed.

In developing the 'core' science skill objectives listed in the two tables, the Group focused entirely on 'science processes' without specifying or referring to specific knowledge items. The advantage of this approach is that it makes the objectives relevant and appropriate for the full spectrum of science activities: teachers can readily adapt them to the various science areas.

Towards an Assessment-led Science Curriculum?

As we have seen, the primary purpose underlying the development of

112

Table 7.5. List of possible performance objectives for the Interpretation and Application area (basic level)

Pupils should show competence in relation to the following:

★ Order simple data and draw a chart, bar graph, line graph or table.

★ Obtain information from a given source, including:
  (a) photographs and drawings,
  (b) symbolic diagrams,
  (c) charts,
  (d) tables,
  (e) bar graphs,
  (f) line graphs,
  (g) passages of information,
  (h) use of an index.

★ Deduce straightforward patterns or relationships in experimental results or presented information.

★ Draw appropriate conclusions from experimental results and from presented information.

★ Make simple predictions from deduced patterns, relationships or conclusions about what might happen in related situations.

★ Decide whether or not a given statement is supported by the given evidence.

Source: Tables 7.5 – 7.7 are based on preliminary information received from the Project on Assessment of Graded Objectives, which is conducted by the Midland Examining Group.
(Note: The Project is located at the University of Cambridge Local Examinations Syndicate.)

Table 7.6. List of performance objectives for the Planning of Experiments area

For a given practical problem for which the apparatus is already provided pupils should:
★ Indicate a course of action to solve the problem.
★ Identify or propose suitable testable statements.
★ Indicate the way in which the apparatus and materials are to be used.
★ Identify possible safety hazards.
★ Identify (i) what to vary, (ii) what to measure, (iii) what to control.
★ Show how to set up initial conditions.
★ Indicate the sequence of activities to be performed.

In addition, for problems where no apparatus is provided, pupils should be able:
★ To indicate the apparatus and materials needed for the investigation.
★ To evaluate the outcomes of an investigation and comment on their validity.

Source: See note to Table 7.5.

criterion-referenced grade descriptions is the establishment of an assessment structure that allows a student's attainment to be judged independently of the attainment profile of the total examined population. However, since these grade descriptions also define the various learning outcomes which students are expected to demonstrate at the end of their course, they must also define – at least implicitly – the purpose of the instruction. By instruction we mean here both the teaching and the learning experiences to which the student is exposed.

The notion that descriptions of objectives (this is basically what the criterion-referenced grade descriptions represent, especially in their elaborated form) serve a dual function in an educational context has long been recognised. Gagné and Briggs, for example, asserted that 'objectives serve as guidelines for developing instruction, and for designing measures of student performance . . . '.[7] The same interrelationship between objectives, instruction and assessment is also generally endorsed by curriculum theorists.[8]

The relationship between objectives and the instructional process merits particular attention. It is a relationship that can be viewed in two different ways. On the one hand, we may argue with Gagné and Briggs that, being informed about objectives, the teacher will be able to decide:

Whether a lesson has a suitable 'balance' of expected outcomes;
and
whether the approach to instruction is matched to the type of objective in each case.

Seen in this way, well-defined objectives should prove to be an aid to the purposeful design of instruction. On the other hand, the possibility exists that the overall purpose of instruction will be viewed by teachers and others solely in terms of a range of prespecified assessment objectives. In consequence, the development of qualities that are not specifically covered by objectives statements would be neglected and even ignored. Thus, any graded objective,[9] initially specified in order to allow the meaningful interpretation of assessment grades, would function as determinants of the content and orientation of instruction and, hence, the curriculum. In other words, the curriculum would be led by assessment objectives.

Already, indications exist that the development of graded objectives in science will have curricular consequences. For example, the Science Curriculum Group of the Midland Examining Group (whose work was referred to above) has drawn up a tentative list of science skills and of suggested activities that can be used to teach these skills. Table 7.7 presents selected samples of these skills and activities proposed for science courses in the 11–13 age range.

The activity examples shown in Table 7.7 refer in the main to science

114

Table 7.7. Examples of science process objectives (for observation skills) and suggested learning activities

Process skill	Suggested learning activities
Observe similarities and differences using: (a) living and non-living things, (b) diagrams, photographs,	Looking at similarities and differences between two objects, using laboratory glassware, materials and other apparatus. Use could be made of live animals and plants as well as photographs and diagrams of either living or non-living things. Activities on grouping things.
(c) sounds,	Audio-tapes could be used to observe similarities and differences between recorded sounds (such as loudness, pitch, duration and rhythm).
(d) readings on scientific apparatus or instruments,	Observations could be made directly from pre-set measuring instruments or apparatus or from diagrams or photographs of them.
(e) written data.	Pupils could be provided with simple descriptions of various chemicals with obvious observable differences. These descriptions could be matched with actual samples. Descriptions could be given of two living or non-living things for comparison. This could be part of an activity on grouping things.
Observe and describe changes in colour.	Practical exercises of demonstrations such as: (a) heating hydrated copper(II) sulphate, (b) adding acids and alkalis to indicators (with a list of colours to choose from).
Identify coloured substances by matching them with reference colours.	Practical work with indicators. Looking for distinct changes. Recognition of shades within a given colour.
Read the scales of appropriate measuring instruments and apparatus and record measurements.	Linear scales with scale divisions of single, whole units should be read correct to one scale division. The correct reading of a measuring cylinder $(0-100 \text{ cm}^3 \times \text{cm}^3)$ correct to one scale division.
Observe possible hazards in a given situation.	Several pictorial representations of scientific activities could be provided, each showing one unsafe practice. The hazard could be identified from a list of five when only one is correct. Other pictures could represent a specified number of obvious hazards that the pupils must identify.

Source: see note to Table 7.5.

processes. By and large, they do not specify the subject matter to be explored through the activities. Decisions about this are left to the teachers. However, as performance objectives are defined for the higher age ranges, increasingly more attention will have to be given to the subject-matter knowledge to be acquired by the students, in addition to the science process skills. This may then well result in a tighter, more prescriptive specification of learning activities than is the case for the lower age group. If this happens, the influence of the graded assessment objectives upon the curriculum will be very pronounced.

That examinations have a distinct effect on the nature and content of school work has long been established. In relation to science education, this was clearly demonstrated by Kerr[10] for practical work and confirmed more recently in the survey of secondary education in England, conducted by HM Inspectorate[11]. The proposed introduction of graded assessment would thus not give rise to a new effect. However, it might well extend the existing effect to the actual learning experiences to which students are exposed, thereby giving rise to a curriculum which is even more assessment-led than is currently the case.

We must view this possibility with considerable concern, for two reasons:

i The aims of science education are more diffuse and wide-ranging than any assessment framework, however detailed and comprehensive, can encompass. In many of its intentions, science education (like education in general) aims at the whole person, and seeks outcomes such as self-fulfilment and the development of attitudes and values. These, frankly, cannot be itemised in terms of specific objectives or descriptions of attainments.

ii However useful and convenient teachers may initially find detailed, specific recommendations for new curricular activities, undue reliance on these would in the long run cause the 'deprofessionalisation' of what is currently one of the best qualified and most innovative science teaching forces in the world.

Assessing Graded Objectives

So far in this chapter, the discussion has focused on the nature and development of graded objectives and on related issues, e.g. the specification of learning activities whereby the learner can be guided to the attainment of these objectives. The issue now to be considered concerns the actual assessment of the skills and competences referred to in graded objectives and the technical problems associated with such assessment.

As with norm-referenced tests, we require criterion-referenced assessment procedures to be both valid and reliable. However, the stringency of this condition in the case of criterion-referenced testing is inevitably higher, since we wish to identify in the student levels of attainment of fairly specific objectives, and not merely place him or her in some rank order position relative to other students. Any item or performance criterion used in criterion-referenced assessment must accurately reflect the objective to which it relates; without this, the item cannot be regarded as valid. However, the use of a single item cannot lead to a confident conclusion that the student has actually mastered the skill or competence implied by the objective. Thus, in order to arrive at a generalisable judgement about a student's attainment level, a number of different occasions or situations has to be provided on which the student can demonstrate quality of performance.

The latter requirement clearly calls for the development, on the part of the assessor or examiner, of a number of different, but 'equivalent' assessment tasks. (The notion of 'equivalence', as used here, implies that the tasks must measure the same skill and allow the same performance levels to be identified.) To what extent, one must ask, can this requirement be met in practice? This issue is to be considered now.

To begin with, it is appropriate to recognise that every examination task may be characterised in terms of three basic qualities:

i The particular abilities or skills which it requires the student to display (task variable).

ii The subject matter with respect to which the skill is to be demonstrated (subject-matter variable).

iii The mode or format in which the task is presented to the student (format variable).

The first two of these aspects are self-explanatory. As regards the mode/format aspect, this may refer to the type of assessment (e.g. whether written, practical or oral, etc.) as well as to the form in which tasks are presented (e.g. the form of multiple-choice, short-answer or essay-type questions). In the present discussion, the format of task presentation only will be considered.

As is readily seen from Tables 7.1 to 7.4, practically all the graded objectives proposed for the new GCSE examination are ability/skills-related. By this is meant that they express the generalised skills and competences that students are expected to display for the award of particular grades. However, the objectives statements do not contain any reference to either the subject-matter content to be covered by the assessment or to the format in which examination tasks are to be presented. Given this situation, one has to raise the question of whether examination tasks or subtasks can validly be assigned to particular skills/ability categories, irrespective of the format in which they appear or the subject matter content with which they are associated.

To answer this question in relation to the subject-matter aspect, it has to be argued that no *a priori* reason exists why the performance at a particular ability level should be uniform across a wide range of subject matter. For example, a student's level of actual knowledge and understanding in one area of biology may well be different from that in another area. This in itself is no obstacle to a meaningful application of criterion-referencing, since it is possible, both in principle and in practice, to 'sample' the student's factual knowledge across a representative range of, say, biological phenomena and from this determine an 'average' performance level for this ability. The same is true for other skills and abilities.

The situation is different for the mode/format aspect. Here, the basic issue is whether, for example, 'recall-type' questions, presented respectively in a multiple-choice or short-answer format, elicit similar responses from students. Unless the answer to this question is affirmative, a characterisation of student attainment simply in terms of abilities or skills is not possible. Instead, a student's response to an examination task would be conditional, at least in part, on the format in which the task is presented. Were this to be the case, the intentions underlying the introduction of criterion-referencing would largely be negated.

The findings from several recent researches suggest that students' performances, as measured by conventional written assessment techniques, are indeed significantly affected by the format of the examination tasks and by the context in which they appear. In one such study,[12] the examination papers of a representative group of A-level Chemistry students were reassessed using a criterion-referenced procedure, and student performances analysed in terms of (a) the abilities and skills, and (b) types of question as they appeared in the different examination papers. The objectives-related part-scores thus obtained were factor-analysed in order to determine the relationship between student performances on different objectives and question types.[13] The results of this analysis are shown in a simplified form in Table 7.8. The ticks indicate how the various ability/skills variables relate to the 'factors' identified.

It is evident from the table that each factor tends to group together variables belonging to a particular examination paper. Thus, factor I is clearly associated with Paper 3; this comprised essay-type questions only, which were analysed in terms of 'recall of factual knowledge' and 'problem-solving' skills, as well as a range of 'communication skills'. Factors II and III correspond to Papers 2 and 1, respectively; of these, Paper 1 consisted entirely of multiple-choice questions, whilst Paper 2 contained only short-answer (structured) questions.

The significant factor of these results, in relation to the issue discussed in this section, is that they do not show any significant commonality across the examination papers of variables expressing the same or similar abilities and skills. For example, students' application (problem-

Table 7.8. Schematic results of factor-analytic study of the relationship between question format and performance in various skill/ability areas

Ability/skill assessed	Strong loading of variables on		
	Factor I	Factor II	Factor III
Paper 1 (Multiple-choice questions)			
Recall and basic knowledge			✓
Comprehension/understanding		(✓)	✓
Application of knowledge			✓
Higher abilities (judgement and evaluation)			✓
Paper 2 (Structured short-answer questions)			
Recall and basic knowledge		✓	
Comprehension/understanding		✓	
Problem-solving (application) skills		✓	
Judgement and evaluation abilities		✓	
Knowledge of experimental procedures and techniques	(✓)	✓	
Knowledge of industrial processes and applied aspects of chemistry		✓	
Paper 3 (Essay-type questions)			
Recall – factual knowledge	✓		
Problem-solving (application) skills	✓		
Clarity of expression*	✓		
Relevance of information*	✓		
Logicality of arguments*	✓		
Sequencing of arguments*	✓		

Abilities marked by an asterisk are components of 'communication' skills.
Ticks in parentheses indicate loadings of variables on a second factor.
Source: Based on an analysis of GCE A-level Chemistry papers.

solving) skills as measured by multiple-choice questions (Paper 1), appear to be largely unrelated to the same skills when they are measured by means of structured questions or as part of essay-type assignments. The general conclusion to be drawn from this is that students' performance on the various ability/skills-related tasks is strongly dependent on the format of task presentation.

Recent results reported by the Science Monitoring teams of the APU confirm the above conclusion.[14] Reviewing pupils' performances on questions demanding the same science process skills to be demonstrated, the teams drew attention to the wide range of mean scores obtained on the questions. Table 7.9 illustrates this for a limited range of skills.

Table 7.9. Student performances on objectives-related assessment tasks in the 'Interpretation of Scientific Information' domain

Ability/skill tested	Number of questions examined	Range of mean scores on questions[a]	Average of mean scores[a]
Description of pattern embedded in presented information	17	5–47	30
Generation of a prediction from given pattern	22	6–69	36
Selection of a prediction (from 4 or more options) on the basis of given pattern	13	11–72	41

[a] Scores are expressed as percentages.
Source: Based on APU findings for 13+ year olds.

The overall conclusion to be drawn from the two sets of research findings presented here is that student performance in an examination cannot be adequately characterised simply in terms of skills and abilities. Student performance of examination-type tasks appears to be far more strongly affected by the format and context of task presentation than by the level of intellectual/cognitive functioning thought to be required for the task.

This finding must cast considerable doubt on the validity, for assessment purposes, of theoretical specifications of expected performance levels, such as those given in Tables 7.1 to 7.4, which refer merely to skills and abilities. In a development of a dependable system of criterion-referenced testing and examining, it is essential that due cognisance is taken of the influences of question format and content on student performance. This, however, makes the grading procedure rather complex and may possibly render it difficult to implement in practice.

Conclusion

The focus in this chapter has been on the move towards criterion-referencing in our public examinations. The case for this move is a very strong one, for two reasons. First, if the move succeeds, candidates will be assessed on the basis of their actual achievements and competences, and not in relation to other candidates, as is largely the case now. Secondly, the adoption of criterion-referencing will require us to define clearly the qualities that we seek to foster in students and the criteria which should be used for their assessment. This in itself is a worthwile activity from an educational point of view.

The development of an operational scheme of criterion-referenced examining poses a number of technical problems that have yet to be solved, but this is an interesting challenge for future work.

Notes and References

1 Sir Keith Joseph 'Address to the North of England Education Conference, Sheffield, 6 January 1984'. Reported in the *Times Educational Supplement*, 13 January 1984, pages 4–5.

2 For example, one such project is conducted by the Midland Examining Group, which was established in 1984 by the following bodies: the Cambridge, Oxford and Southern School Examinations Council, the East Midland Regional Examinations Board and the West Midlands Examinations Board.

3 Scottish Examination Board *Standard Grade: Arrangements in Science at Foundation, General and Credit Level* Scottish Examination Board (Edinburgh) 1984.

4 The GCSE provides for seven 'pass' grades, ranging from A to G. The relationship between these grades and the grades available under GCE O-level/CSE system is shown in Table 9.1 (page 134).

5 Department of Education and Science (DES) *GCSE (General Certificate of Secondary Education) – the National Criteria* HMSO (London) 1985.

6 Scottish Examination Board, see note 3 above.

7 R.M. Gagné and L.J. Briggs *Principles of Instructional Design* Holt, Reinhart and Winston (New York) 1974.

8 See, for example, J.F. Kerr 'The problem of curriculum reform' in J.F. Kerr *Changing the Curriculum* University of London Press (London) 1968 pages 13–38.

9 Graded objectives of the type currently under development will correspond to a progressive sequence of attainment from the lowest to the highest level. It is the range of skills, abilities and competences associated with the latter that will be interpreted as the objectives of a course or curriculum, notwithstanding the fact that not all students would be expected to reach this level.

10 J.F. Kerr *Practical Work in School Science* Leicester University Press (Leicester) 1964.

11 DES *Aspects of Secondary Education in England: A Survey by H.M. Inspectors of Schools* HMSO (London) 1979.

12 R.F. Kempa and J. L'Odiaga 'Criterion-referenced interpretation of examination grades.' *Educational Research*, Volume 26 (1984) pages 56–64.

13 Factor-analysis is a statistical technique by which the 'commonality' or connectedness of variables can be examined. Variables that share some common determinant appear together in one and the same 'factor'.

14 DES *Science in Schools. Age 13: Report No. 4* Department of Education and Science (London) 1984.

8

Profiles and Profiling

In recent years, increasing attention has been given to the issue of how the results of examinations and assessments can be expressed and communicated in a meaningful and informative way. The reason for this lies in the realisation that the single grades that are conventionally used to summarise examination and assessment results provide little information about the qualities that are reflected in them. Not surprisingly, therefore, other modes of communicating assessment results have been advocated, foremost among them the use of 'profiles'.

In its simplest form, a profile is a document that presents information about a student's performance over a range of different skills and abilities. Usually these skills and abilities are those that the student's course sought to develop. More elaborate profiles may also cover certain non-academic features, such as the attitudes and personal attributes of the student.

The general intention underlying the use of profiles is to provide as comprehensive a picture of a student's qualities as can be justified in terms of the assessments made. Provided that these qualities are so chosen that they allow a meaningful characterisation of the student's abilities and attainments, etc., the information recorded in profiles should be readily interpretable by, for example, potential employers, institutes of higher education and others. It could be left to these 'consumers' of profiles to decide for themselves on the relative importance of the various qualities covered by a profile.

If the greater information-content that profiles have compared with conventional single grades is one argument in their favour, there is at least one other: students' achievements and abilities are essentially multi-dimensional, i.e. they comprise a range of independent facets. This is illustrated, for example, in a study by Vincent in which he examined students' performances on the components of a college-based chemistry examination and found three discrete, independent performance factors to emerge:[1]

i Performance on three theory papers (written papers dealing with the theoretical, non-practical aspects of chemistry).

ii Performance in practical examination (formally conducted under normal examination conditions).

iii Course work performance, derived from a system of continuous assessment.

Given the independence of these factors, there is clearly no justification for combining scores obtained by students on them into single overall grades. Such 'overall grades' would lack interpretability and meaning. Consider, for example, a hypothetical situation where assessments relating to two independent qualities, X and Y, are combined on the basis of equal weightings. What, under these circumstances, would an overall mark of, say 50% mean? Would it denote a situation where the student is judged to be average with respect to both qualities, X and Y? Or would it denote a situation where high achievement in X is accompanied by low attainment in Y, or vice versa? It is evident that the single grade provides no information about this.

This view is strongly supported by Rowntree, who argues:

Whatever the span [of knowledge, skills and experiences] encompassed [by assessments], a profile . . . helps to humanise the reporting response. Even the simplest of profiles differentiates the student from other students who share the 'same' total, but 'add up' differently from him.[2]

Rowntree's reference to the humanising effect of profiling on the totality of the assessment procedure is particularly noteworthy. This sentiment is widely shared and represents yet a further argument in favour of profiling.

Some Technical Issues

Profiling is as yet a relatively undeveloped technique in the general area of assessments and examinations. Not surprisingly, therefore, it gives rise to a number of technical issues and problems. These fall into two broad categories:

i Those relating to the nature of profiles, their format and the qualities to be described in them, etc.

ii Those concerned with the technical aspects of the educational measurements on which profiles are based, including the issue of profile validity and reliability.

Some of these issues are discussed in the following sections.

The Nature and Format of Profiles

The attractiveness of profiles lies in the fact that they can provide more extensive and, it is hoped, more useful information about individual students than do conventional assessments grades. It has been argued that this information to be contained in profiles can be of two different kinds:

i It can simply represent an extension of conventional (norm-referenced) assessment and examination procedures, in the sense that student performance is reported on a larger number of dimensions than is the case in ordinary examination practice.
ii The information presented is a record of the student's abilities, skills and attitudes, etc., which are explicitly stated and describe the student's characteristics and attributes on a criterion-referenced basis.

It is immediately apparent that the value of profiles of the second kind is likely to be much greater than that of the first kind. However, it must also be said that their development is intrinsically more difficult, for the reasons identified, in Chapter 7, in connection with criterion-referenced testing in general.

Early attempts to develop operational profiles focused in the main on the range of skills and abilities to be acquired by the student. For example, a profiling scheme by Kempa and Ongley for use in university science courses covered the following areas:[3]

- knowledge of basic facts;
- ability to apply knowledge;
- calculative and mathematical competence;
- deductive/reasoning ability;
- basic practical skills;
- design/execution of practical investigations;
- persistence and application in practical work;
- ability to work independently;
- communication skills.

Such a scheme is relatively simple and, hence, superficially attractive. However, its major disadvantage is that it seeks to 'summarise' students' performances across different branches of the subject, disregarding the fact that these may vary significantly from branch to branch.

The non-uniformity in performance over different subject areas frequently observed in students is a strong argument against the use of simple, relatively unsophisticated profiling schemes. Not surprisingly, therefore, recent developments in profiling have given rise to fairly intricate and complex schemes. For example, a profile report form developed by the City and Guilds of London Institute for its Vocational Preparation programme covers four main elements:

1 Attainment and Basic Skills – comprising 14 subcategories of skills to be assessed.
2 Examples of Basic Abilities demonstrated by student in his studies – to be recorded by teaching team.
3 List of typical learning experiences that reflect the activities carried out by the student – to be recorded by the course tutors.

4 Additional reports to 'complete the picture of the student's achievement and experience throughout the course', relating to extension studies, work experience, etc.

The profile report form itself extends over four A4 pages, fairly closely printed and this is indicative of the complexity of the scheme.

Examples of approaches different from the development and presentation of profile report forms are given below.

Qualities for Inclusion in Profiles

The issue of what qualities should be recorded in a profile is crucial in as much as on it will hinge the acceptability of a profile to the interest groups concerned with it, viz. teachers, students, and employers or other 'users' of profiles. Each of these groups is bound to view the acceptability of profiles from its own vantage point: teachers will endeavour to restrict the qualities referred to in a profile to those that they feel able to assess effectively and that they are prepared to assess on, for example, ethical grounds; students may be reluctant to see profiles issued that extend beyond a recording of qualities that relate directly to their educational programme; employers and others may not find profiles useful unless they provide the kind of information needed by them for their particular purpose.

As part of their study, Kempa and Ongley sampled the views of teachers, students and employers on the range of qualities to be included in profiles, with the following results:

i There was general agreement among the three groups that profiles should report not only academic qualities, but also certain non-academic qualities. The latter, it was suggested, should be those that relate fairly closely to a student's (academic) performance or have a bearing on it.

ii The case for the inclusion of non-academic qualities in profiles was particularly strongly supported by the potential employers of students: they stressed the value of such information for personnel selection and placement. Among the non-cognitive qualities mentioned as desirable were: motivation, enthusiasm, ability to get on with people, potential for management and personality. It has to be admitted, though, that few employers were able to suggest how these qualities could be reliably assessed and adequately described in profiles.

The foregoing finding is in full agreement with the conclusions reached in a research project on profile assessment that was carried out during the period 1972–1977, under the auspices of the Scottish Council for Research in Education.[4] In relation to employers' views on profiles, the researchers state:

Reaction [to profiling] was generally favourable. .... The plan to record assessments of basic skills and certain non-cognitive factors like Perseverance and

Enterprise was welcomed as useful, although for some jobs it was felt academic achievement was likely to remain the main criterion . . . . Clear and brief observations of non-cognitive characteristics too were felt to be equally important since for other pupils factors such as the ability to get on with people were more important than subject attainment.

The Research Group reports a similar attitude on the part of higher education. For example, colleges of education are stated as welcoming profiles, since they would 'help their selection procedures in so far as they were looking for qualities other than purely academic ability'.

Of crucial importance in reaching decisions about the content of profiles are the views of teachers as the persons responsible for making and collating the assessments to feature (or not to feature) in profiles. As the Scottish research study was able to establish, teachers appear to endorse the inclusion in profiles of a wide range of cognitive characteristics that may relate to the students' basic skills and abilities as well as to their actual attainment. As regards non-cognitive characteristics, the following were most frequently recommended for inclusion in profiles: Interest, Perseverance, Reliability and Effort; by comparison, Social Competence, Leadership and Friendliness were advocated by only a minority of teachers.

The foregoing teachers' views (which coincide largely with those held by university science lecturers in the Kempa and Ongley study) led to the following conclusions:

i Extensive consensus exists about the inclusion in profiles of a full range of cognitive qualities. These may relate to the students' skills and abilities, as well as to their attainments.
ii The coverage in profiles of non-cognitive characteristics is also generally supported, provided that they are sufficiently 'work-related' in nature. An extension of profiles to, for example, personal attributes is not deemed desirable by teachers and students.

Profile Validity and Reliability

The overall quality of a profile can only be as high as is the quality of the constituent assessments that it embraces. Each component assessment should therefore be characterised by both high validity and high reliability (cf. Chapter 3). In the case of assessment profiles, this requirement is significantly more important than in situations where part-marks are combined to produce uni-dimensional grades, so that errors in the assessment of one component can be masked by the quality of the other assessments.

All the observations made in Chapter 3 about the validity and reliability of assessments do naturally apply to assessment profiles also. However, two additional points are noteworthy:

i For the components to feature in a profile to be assessable and interpretable in a *valid* and meaningful way, it is essential to specify and describe clearly the constructs and criteria that are associated with each assessed component. This requirement is particularly important in relation to non-cognitive characteristics and attributes for which no agreed 'standards' are available.

ii An adequate specification of assessment criteria also promotes the consistency (reliability) of any assessment made, both between different assessment occasions and between different assessors. It also reduces the subjectivity sometimes associated with assessments, which leads to impressions gained of one area of the student's performance to be 'transferred' to another. For example, good achievement is judged to be the consequence of the learner's effort and motivation, which are, thus, also judged to be high.

Commenting on the relative importance of the validity and the reliability issue in relation to profiling, Mackintosh makes the interesting observation that

the across-the-board emphasis on profiles should be upon validity and not upon reliability although this ought not to mean . . . that reliability in relation to the recording [of assessments] is an insignificant issue.[5]

This would place the main stress on the first point above and make it the main issue to which teachers and others concerned with profiles and profiling should address themselves.

Profiles in Practice

The concept of profiling in the context of normal examinations, e.g. at school and college level, is of fairly recent origin. Consequently, few examples are available as yet of fully operational profiles and none of these refers specifically to the science domain.

Early attempts to develop profiles involved little more than an extension of the norm-referenced assessments used in public examinations to a range of different qualities. For example, in the development project on profiling undertaken by the Scottish Council for Research in Education,[6] schools were asked to grade their students' cognitive characteristics on a 1 to 5 scale, aiming at a grade distribution of 10, 20, 40, 20 and 10 % of their total group.

A similar grading procedure was used by Kempa and Ongley in their study of profiling in university level chemistry courses.[7] However, instead of specifying a grade distribution pattern to be obtained, they defined their grades as follows: 5 = excellent, very good; 3 = average; 1 = poor, weak, distinctly below average. The reference in these grade descriptions to 'average' underlines their norm-referenced approach.

It is true that norm-referenced profiles have the advantage of informing the user about the range and variety of qualities on which the student was assessed. However, unless the user is adequately informed about the characteristics of the population group with reference to which the student was assessed, this kind of profile is difficult to interpret. Consequently, preference has to be given to criterion-referenced profiles.

A number of these has emerged in recent years, chiefly in connection with the development of vocational and pre-vocational courses. Some of these are illustrated in Figs. 8.1 to 8.3. Figure 8.1 represents a profile report form for the assessment of students' 'basic skills' developed in a Technician Studies course. It was originally designed for use with Technician Education Council (now Business and Technician Education Council) courses. The areas assessed on the form are self-explanatory, but it should be noted that for their assessment a semantic differential technique has been adopted.

The second example, shown in Fig. 8.2, represents a section of a profile report form issued by the City and Guilds of London Institute for its 365 Vocational Preparation (General) programme. This particular section is used to record students' achievements in Practical and Numerical Abilities and is one of four sections in the report that is generally concerned with attainment in Basic Abilities (the others are Social Abilities, Communication, and Decision-Making Abilities). It is seen that for each particular skill/ability four different levels of attainment are identified. As each of these attainment levels is demonstrated by the student, the small strip at the bottom of each ability subcategory is to be shaded in up to the level achieved, and dated. In this way, a record of the student's progress is shown, with information about the final attainment.

The final example is given in Fig. 8.3 (a) to (c). It represents an illustration of the School Leaver's Attainment Profile of Numerical Skills (SLAPONS), which was originally developed by the Shell Centre of Mathematical Education of the University of Nottingham. The SLAPONS profile is used to record the attainments of individual school leavers in 18 numerical skills (see Fig. 8.3 (a)). These attainments can then be compared by a prospective employer with his own minimum requirements (which may vary with the particular job for which the young school leaver is considered), using the template procedure shown in Fig. 8.3(b) and (c). In this way, the applicant's profile can be used to identify whether his or her numerical skills are adequate for the job, or whether there are weaknesses in numerical achievement which, if the person is otherwise suitable, would have to be remedied.

These examples give but a small indication of the variety of profiles that can be thought of in order to allow students' attainments and abilities to be recorded and communicated in a meaningful way. They were chosen because between them they illustrate how information about students' attainments or abilities can be recorded in a numerical, verbal and graphical format, respectively. Which of these communication modes is to be preferred depends ultimately on the clarity with which profiles can be interpreted by those who use them.

Fig. 8.1 Profile form relating to the assessment of 'Basic Skills' in Technician Studies courses.
Source: **Reported in Further Education Curriculum Review and Development Unit** *Profiles* **Department of Education and Science (London) 1982.**

TECHNICIAN EDUCATION COUNCIL
Profile Statement for a Course in Technician Studies
Basic Skills

Student:

College: Date:

The following summarises some of the basic skills of the above student at an early stage in the course. The document is intended to provide a basis for consideration of the course most appropriate to the student. The profile is in the form of two opposite statements with the position of the student between those extremes being indicated in a five-point scale.

	1	2	3	4	5	
1. Communicates easily with others (a) Reads fluently with understanding. (b) Can express ideas clearly in writing.						1. Has difficulty in communicating clearly with others. (a) Reads with difficulty and finds difficulty in understanding what is read. (b) Finds difficulty in expressing ideas clearly in writing.
2. Uses mathematics without difficulty. (a) Carries out basic arithmetical operations with ease. (b) Has no problems with fractions and decimals.						2. Prefers to avoid situations involving mathematics. (a) Has great difficulty with basic arithmetic. (b) Has difficulty with mathematics involving fractions and decimals.
3. Develops manipulative skills quickly. (a) Able to use basic workshop tools/laboratory equipment. (b) Produces clear drawings/ sketches.						3. Takes a lot of practice to develop manipulative skills. (a) Has difficulty in using workshop tools/laboratory equipment. (b) Has difficulty in producing clear drawings/sketches.
4. Methodical						4. Haphazard in approach to problems.
5. Self-reliant						5. Needs constant supervision.

The student has carried out assignments and visits relating to the following industrial sectors:
Engineering; Construction; Science; Hotel Catering and Institutional Management; ....

....

(Delete inapplicable sectors; include additional sectors as appropriate.)

General Comments:

Fig. 8.2 Profile section on 'Practical and Numerical Abilities', as part of the City and Guilds of London Institute's profile on Attainments in Basic Abilities.

Source: Reported in Further Education Curriculum Review and Development Unit *Profiles* Department of Education and Science (London) 1982.

Level of attainment

	4 (Basic level)	3	2	1 (High level)
Using equipment	After demonstration, can use equipment safely to perform simple tasks.	With guidance can use equipment safely to perform multi-step tasks.	Can select and use suitable equipment and materials for the job without help.	Can set up and maintain equipment. Can identify/ remedy common faults.
Dexterity and coordination	Can use everyday implements, can lift, carry and set down objects as directed.	Can reliably perform basic manipulative tasks.	Can perform complex tasks requiring accuracy and dexterity.	Can perform tasks requiring a high degree of manipulative control.
Measuring	Can read graduated linear scales and dials.	Can measure out specified quantities of material by length, weight, etc.	Can set up and use simple precision instruments.	Can set up and use complex precision instruments.
Calculating	Can identify size, shape, order, etc. Can add and subtract whole numbers.	Can use $+/-/\times/\div$ to solve single-step, whole number problems. Can estimate.	Can use $+/-/\times/\div$ to solve two-step problems. Can add and subtract decimals.	Can use $+/-/\times/\div$ to solve multi-step problems. Can multiply and divide decimals.

Fig. 8.3 Examples of SLAPONS (School Leaver's Attainment Profile of Numerical Skills), developed by the Shell Centre of Mathematical Education, University of Nottingham. N, natural (whole) numbers; F, fractions; D, decimals; REL, related thinking; APP, approximations; EST, estimations.

Source: Adapted from Further Education Curriculum Review and Development Unit *Profiles* Department of Education and Science (London) 1982.

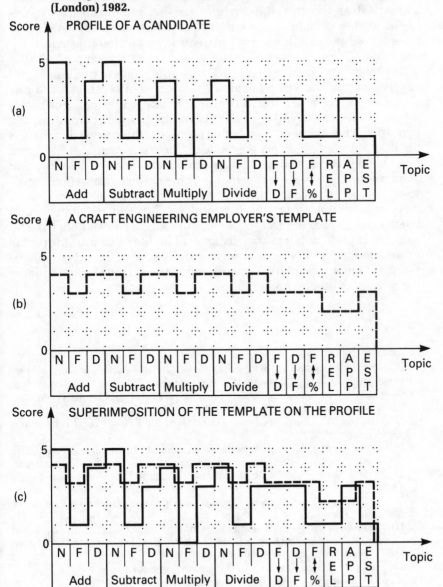

Conclusion

The considerable interest in profiling that has emerged in recent years is largely the result of the inadequacy of the information that is conveyed by conventional examination grades. Such grades frequently mask the diversity of a student's achievement and performance in different ability and skill areas. By contrast, a carefully designed profile can give a meaningful picture of the student's strengths and weaknesses, which is of potential value to employers, parents, education and training personnel, and others. The case for profiling thus becomes a strong one.

At present, the number of operational applications of profiling is still relatively small and largely confined to the area of vocational and pre-vocational education within the Further Education sector. The Further Education sector, it should be noted, is a sector in which currently major educational developments are taking place, and this obviously provides the opportunity for innovative work in the assessment area also. One must hope that innovations such as profiling will also be taken up and explored by the school sector in due course. The examination boards would have a key role in this.

As pointed out above, the issues of validity and reliability are of crucial importance in profiling – more so than in conventional assessments. It is perhaps fair to state that not all problems concerning profile validity and reliability have as yet been fully solved, but this should be taken as a challenge for further work and not as a reason for abandoning the concept of profiles and profiling.

Notes and References

1 A. Vincent 'Chemical ability or chemical abilities – a study of some assessment procedures' in R. Kempa, D.E. Hoare and R.J.D. Rutherford *Research in Assessment* The Chemical Society [now Royal Society of Chemistry] Assessment Group (London) 1975 pages 69–76.

2 D. Rowntree *Assessing Students – How Shall We Know Them?* Harper and Row (London) 1977.

3 R.F. Kempa and P.A. Ongley *Profile Assessment in Chemistry: A Feasibility Study into the Multi-dimensional Reporting of Attainment in Chemistry in University Level Courses* Department of Education (University of Keele) 1979.

4 Scottish Council for Research in Education *Pupils in Profile* Hodder & Stoughton (London) 1977.

5 H. Mackintosh 'A 17+ package: a view from the school' in Further Education Curriculum Review and Development Unit *Profiles* Department of Education and Science (London) 1982 pages 51–9.

6 Scottish Council for Research in Education, see note 4 above.

7 R.F. Kempa and P.A. Ongley, see note 3 above.

9

Issues for the Future

This book has attempted to give a brief, though informative picture of contemporary practices and current trends in the examination and assessment area. Thus, we have reviewed and discussed procedures and techniques available for the assessment of a wide range of abilities, skills and affective qualities that science education seeks to foster in students. We have also considered the moves, currently under way, towards criterion-referencing in examinations and profiling. As was seen, the latter two areas are not without problems, but it may confidently be expected that these will in due course be satisfactorily solved through further research and development work.

Currently, much of the debate about examinations centres on the introduction, in 1988, of the new GCSE examination system which will take the place of the separate GCE O-level and CSE examinations (see Chapter 1). The broad framework for this new examination has already been established and is described in relevant publications issued by the Department of Education and Science. Among the requirements for the GCSE are the following:

i It will be a single system of examinations, with a single scale of grades, for the total ability range of pupils who are currently covered by the O-level and CSE examinations. In practice, this is the upper 60% of the total school population at age 16+, at least for science.

ii All GCSE courses and examinations will have to follow sets of 'national criteria'[1] that specify the objectives, content areas and examination procedures appropriate for the various subjects in the curriculum. One consequence of this will be that the traditional mode of differentiating between high-ability and less able pupils by assigning them to different courses (e.g. 'academic' and 'non-academic') will no longer be possible.

Both requirements, taken together, pose a significant problem for the consortia of examining boards that have been charged with the responsibility of setting GCSE examinations and awarding grades. They have to develop a unified examination structure that will allow a proper discrimination to be achieved among candidates who, in terms of ability and performance, will be far more diverse than is currently the case for the separate examinations. This particular problem is considered below.

Examinations of the 16+ age stage are, of course, only part of the English system of public examinations. This also includes the GCE

A-level examinations and examinations, such as the Alternative Ordinary level examinations of the GCE boards, which are intermediate between O-level and A-level examinations. In view of the forthcoming change in the 16+ examination structure, we may also enquire what changes, if any, are envisaged for the examination structure for the post-16 age range. This matter is also discussed below.

Differentiated Assessments

According to the general principles and requirement governing the new GCSE examinations:

all examinations must be designed in such a way as to ensure proper discrimination so that candidates across the [full] ability range are given opportunities to demonstrate their knowledge, abilities and achievements.[2]

Given the fact that the ability and achievement spectrum of GCSE candidates will be considerably wider than that for the current, separate examinations in the O-level/CSE system, one has to ask whether it is technically possible to achieve such 'proper discrimination' by means of a single set of examination papers.

In relation to the sciences (and a range of other subjects), the firm view has emerged that single sets of papers that would be common to *all* GCSE candidates could not produce the desired discrimination. It is claimed that, if papers sought to distinguish between performance levels at the 'top end' of the achievement spectrum, they would fail to produce an adequate discrimination among candidates in the bottom region of the performance spectrum. The reverse would be true if an extensive discrimination of candidates at the bottom end were sought: in this case, the set of papers would not discriminate at the top end of the performance spectrum.

The nature of this problem is readily appreciated when the relationship between grades in the new GCSE system and the O-level/CSE structure is considered (cf. Table 9.1). It is seen that GCSE examinations will have to be capable of distinguishing between eight levels of performance (which includes the 'ungraded' level).

Table 9.1. Relationship between grades for GCSE, GCE O-level and CSE examinations

O-level grades	A	B	C	D	E	—	—
GCSE grades	A	B	C	D	E	F	G
CSE grades		1		2	3	4	5

To overcome this problem, the use of differentiated assessments has been advocated. In this, candidates would be offered, within each subject, a choice of papers (or questions within papers). Papers (or questions) that may be taken as alternatives would differ in their degree of difficulty, with the more difficult versions aiming at high ability candidates and the easier ones aiming at students at the lower end of the performance spectrum.

Table 9.2 gives an example of a provisional GCSE assessment scheme for a science subject. It is seen that Paper 1 is a 'common' paper, i.e. it is to be taken by all GCSE candidates in the given subject, whereas Papers 2 and 3 are alternatives. In the case of this particular example, Paper 2 is meant for candidates likely to achieve GCSE grades in the range C to G, whilst Paper 3 aims at candidates likely to achieve grades in the A to D range.

Table 9.2. Example of a scheme of differentiated assessment for a GCSE science examination. (a) Description of papers, (b) combination of papers possible

(a) Paper 1	Paper 2	Paper 3
Multiple-choice paper comprising 50 compulsory questions. Duration of paper 1 hour.	To consist of two sections: Section A contains short-answer questions; Section B contains a limited number of structured questions. All questions are compulsory. Duration of paper: 2 hours.	To consist of two sections: Section A contains a limited number of compulsory structured questions; Section B contains five extended-answer questions, of which three have to be attempted. Duration of paper: 2 hours.

(b) Combination	GCSE grade range normally available	Groups of candidates aimed at
Paper 1 and Paper 2	C–G	Average and below average
Paper 1 and Paper 3	A–D	Above average

There is a variety of different ways in which the notion of a differentiated assessment structure can be developed into firm schemes of assessment. At the moment, this development work is still under way and, hence, no evaluation is possible of the effectiveness of such schemes. However, one can foresee a number of issues and problems that may arise from the use of differentiated assessment schemes, which will require careful consideration in due course. Among them are these:

i Will it be possible in practice to establish a meaningful relationship between marks gained by candidates on alternative papers (or questions) so that appropriate equivalences between grades can be deduced? Can we ensure an adequate comparability of marks obtained on the more 'difficult' paper (or combination of papers) and those gained on the 'easier' one? (The role of a common paper (or common questions) may be crucial in this.)

ii Assuming that the differentiation in the assessment is brought about by the use of alternative papers (rather than alternative questions within papers), how can we ensure that candidates make a wise choice of papers or combinations of papers?

The first of these issues is clearly one for examining boards to solve, and may well require considerable research and development work to be done. However, it is an issue that is of paramount importance if the new examination system is to gain credibility and acceptance. It has also a significant bearing on how teachers can respond to the second issue: they would wish to be assured that, whatever option of papers they may recommend to their students, it will provide them with a fair assessment of their skills and abilities.

The Future of Post-16 Examinations

It is the declared policy of the Department of Education and Science that the standards of the new GCSE examination will be at least as high as those of the examinations that it replaces. Given this, there is no obvious reason why the introduction of the GCSE examinations should have any effect on the nature of GCE A-level courses and examinations. Indeed, the Government has openly committed itself to keeping A-levels, and this will ensure that universities and other institutions of higher education will continue to rely on students' A-level achievements as a criterion for selection and admission to degree courses.

Outside the narrow confines of the A-level structure, a number of changes in the post-16 examination structure have recently been put forward in a Government White Paper[3] that, if they are ultimately agreed to, will require much further development work in the area of examinations and assessments.

The Government envisages the introduction, in due course, of two new examinations. The first of these is to be available from 1989 onwards and will be known as Advanced Supplementary (AS) level examination. It is intended to broaden the sixth-form curriculum without reducing standards. Courses leading to AS level examinations will require approximately half the study period needed for an A-level course but, to quote from the DES White Paper,

the general quality of work demanded for the award of any grade will be comparable with that of A-level courses, so that full credit may be given to AS level success in higher education admission successes.

The second new examination will lead to the Certificate of Pre-Vocational Education (CPVE), which is a post-16 qualification for those not pursuing A-levels or other 'academic' courses. As the title of the new qualification suggests, CPVE courses will have a significant vocational element, in addition to providing students with a general and practical education. Details about this new proposed examination have yet to be worked out and, until this has been achieved, no comments can be made about its nature and organisation. What can be said, though, is that this new examination should contribute considerably to a rationalisation of the current diversity of 'non-academic' (i.e. non-A-level) examinations and qualifications in the post-16 education phase. As the White Paper states, CPVE courses should replace a range of existing courses, including the pre-vocational courses of the City and Guilds of London Institute, the Business and Technician Education Council and the Royal Society of Arts, and the Certificate of Extended Education courses currently offered by most CSE and some GCE boards.

Concluding Comments

Much of what has been stated in this and the preceding chapters demonstrates clearly that, as far as examinations and assessment issues are concerned, our situation is far from static. The current transition in the secondary sector from the GCE O-level/CSE structure to the GCSE system is only one of several significant changes in our overall examination structure.

Changes as we witness them are not simply confined to our examination system, they also affect our own practices in conducting assessments and examinations. The move towards criterion-referencing, the advocacy of profiling, including the development of 'records of achievement', the increasing participation of schools and teachers in external examinations, all these are examples of major innovations in the way in which we approach the task of assessing our students.

Without doubt, we shall see further changes and innovations as time passes. We shall have to adjust to these and develop new skills to cope with them. Thus, the current state of affairs can only be temporary, just as any book which, like this one, seeks to describe the contemporary assessment and examinations scene, will before long require revision and updating.

Notes and References

1 In the science area, National Criteria have been published for Biology, Chemistry and Physics, in addition to Science itself. For other science subjects, e.g. Engineering Science, Geology, Materials Science, Rural Science, etc., syllabuses have to comply with the national criteria for Science.

2 Department of Education and Science (DES) *GCSE (General Certificate of Secondary Education) – The National Criteria* HMSO (London) 1985.

3 DES *Better Schools*. Government White Paper 9469 HMSO (London) 1985.

FURTHER READING

Broadfoot, P. (ed.) *Selection, Certification and Control* The Falmer Press (Lewes, Sussex) 1984.
Some 13 contributions from different eminent authors have been brought together in this book. Among them, they explore a wide range of contemporary issues and perspectives concerning examinations, especially their societal functions and roles.

Further Education Unit *Profiles* 1982 and *Profiles in Action* 1984 Department of Education and Science (London).
These publications, which are available from the Publications Despatch Centre of the Department of Education and Science, present a collection of useful and interesting papers on a variety of issues relating to profiling and profile assessment.

Ingle, R. and Jennings A. *Science in Schools: Which Way Now?* University of London Institute of Education (London) 1981.
Although this book does not discuss any issues directly related to assessment and examinations in science, it presents a detailed and well-balanced account of the aims and ideals in science education. These are, of course, of major importance in that they must form the background to any valid system of examinations.

Macintosh H.G. (ed.) *Techniques and Problems of Assessment.* London: Edward Arnold (London) 1974.
This book, edited by the Secretary of a major CSE Board in England, provides a wide-ranging overview of contemporary techniques of assessment and problems associated with them. The book is very appropriately described as 'a practical handbook for teachers'.

Montgomery, R.J. *Examinations* Longmans, Green & Co. (London) 1965.
This book presents an authoritative and comprehensive account of the evaluation of public examinations in England up to the institution of the Certificate of Secondary Education in the early sixties.

Satterley, D. *Assessment in Schools* Blackwell (Oxford) 1981.
This is a very useful text exploring all major aspects of assessment in the context of school education.

Scottish Council for Research in Education *Pupils in Profile* Hodder & Stoughton (London) 1977.
This book reports the findings of a major research study undertaken in Scotland, but touches upon a wide range of issues that is of general concern to those interested in profile assessment.

Scottish Education Department *What do they know? A Review of Criterion-Referenced Assessment* HMSO (Edinburgh) 1980.
This book reports a detailed and scholarly study on criterion-referenced testing and examination that was conducted by Dr Sally Brown on behalf of the Scottish Education Department.

Ward, C. *Preparing and Using Objective Questions* Stanley Thornes (Cheltenham) 1981.
Although written primarily for the Further Education sector, this book provides valuable guidance to all teachers on the writing and editing of objective questions and on the design of objective examinations in general.

SUBJECT INDEX

NAME INDEX